FAVORITE BOARD GAMES YOU CAN MAKE AND PLAY

Asterie Baker Provenzo
and
Eugene F. Provenzo, Jr.

ILLUSTRATIONS AND
PLAYING-BOARD ADAPTATIONS BY

Peter A. Zorn, Jr.

DOVER PUBLICATIONS, INC., New York

Copyright © 1981 by Asterie Baker Provenzo and Eugene F. Provenzo, Jr.
All rights reserved under Pan American and International Copyright
Conventions.

Published in Canada by General Publishing Company, Ltd., 30 Lesmill
Road, Don Mills, Toronto, Ontario.
Published in the United Kingdom by Constable and Company, Ltd.,
3 The Lanchesters, 162–164 Fulham Palace Road, London W6 9ER.

This Dover edition, first published in 1990, is an unabridged, unaltered
republication of the work first published by Prentice-Hall, Inc., Englewood
Cliffs, N.J. ("A Spectrum Book"), 1981, under the title *Play It Again: Historic
Board Games You Can Make and Play.*

Manufactured in the United States of America
Dover Publications, Inc., 31 East 2nd Street, Mineola, N.Y. 11501

Library of Congress Cataloging in Publication Data

Provenzo, Asterie Baker.
    [Play it again]
    Favorite board games you can make and play / by Asterie Baker Provenzo
and Eugene F. Provenzo, Jr. ; illustrations and playing-board adaptations by
Peter A. Zorn, Jr.
        p.   cm.
    Reprint. Originally published: Play it again. Englewood Cliffs, N.J. :
Prentice-Hall. c1981.
    Includes bibliographical references.
    ISBN 0-486-26410-6
    1. Board games. 2. Board games—History. I. Provenzo, Eugene F.
II. Zorn, Peter A. III. Title.
GV1312.P76 1990
794—dc20   90-33761
                                                               CIP

To the memory of our grandfathers,
Bill Sprow, Morris Kutner, and June Baker,
who always found the time to play it again.

CONTENTS

viii

ix

DRAUGHTS.
195

BACKGAMMON.
219

ACKNOWLEDGMENTS

Our thanks go to the many people whose interest and help have contributed to the writing of this book. Important assistance in collecting visual materials and the histories of many of the board games was provided by the librarians and staff of the Newberry Library, Chicago; the Regenstein Library, University of Chicago; Olin Library, Washington University in St. Louis; Sterling and Beinecke Libraries, Yale University; and the United States Patent Office.

Our special thanks go to Bernard Reilly, Library of Congress; Patricia Pardo, Interlibrary Loan Office, Richter Library, University of Miami; Julanne Good and R. David Weaver, St. Louis Public Library; Susan Heintzelman, Teachers College Library, Columbia University; John Thomas, Yale Center for British Art; Wanda Slayton, Ft. Lauderdale, Florida; Lee Dennis, Peterborough, New Hampshire; Herb Siegel, Wyncote, Pennsylvania; and Eric Newman, Prentice-Hall, Inc.

Asterie Baker, Ann and Steven Freedman, and Shep Sporel, as always, were generous with their hospitality and their interest in our project.

INTRODUCTION

Play It Again[*] is a book about some of the most popular board games from both ancient and modern times. It is a book about their history, how to play them, and how to make their boards and playing pieces. As you turn the pages of this book, the historical illustrations, the rules, the boards themselves, and the descriptions of the games will give you the opportunity to explore more than just the world of games—you will become familiar with the history of different cultures and peoples and with the art of gamesmanship.

Almost all board games are imitations of situations in real life. Some depict moral themes; one example of this is the Royal Game of Goose, a race game in which fortunes change suddenly as you land on different squares representing the trials and rewards of life. The role of good luck and bad luck is even more dramatic in Snakes and Ladders. By simply landing on the head of the snake on square 97, your piece must slip all the way back down the snake's body to square eight! Both of these games reflect beliefs about luck and life and were often used to teach children moral lessons about the relationships between good and evil.

Board games have also been used to teach children basic facts and information about the world in which they live. Numerous games from the eighteenth and nineteenth centuries, such as The Mansion of Happiness or An Eccentric Excursion to the Chinese Empire, were used to teach morals, geography, the natural sciences, mathematics, and history. Sometimes the names of board games or even the playing pieces themselves reflected a specific historical event or personage. For

---

*This book was originally published under the title *Play It Again*. Apart from the title change, nothing has been altered in this Dover reprint [1990 note].

example, during the Indian Mutiny of 1857–58, a variation of Fox and Geese known as Asalto was updated to "Officers and Sepoys."

Other board games involve the strategic maneuvers most closely associated with warfare. Chess is a classic example of a game that imitates the basic elements of the battlefield in which players are equally matched. Although Chess is excluded from this book because of its complexity, many other battle games, such as Draughts, Alquerque, and Nine Men's Morris, are included that recreate the excitement of out-maneuvering and out-witting your opponent.

Fox and Geese and the Chinese Rebel Game are examples of another type of battle game or "hunt" in which unequal forces with different capabilities are pitted against each other. Some games, like Reversi or Go-Bang, stress the strategic positioning of your playing pieces. In these games, based solely on skill, it is the placement of pieces and the manipulation of your opponent that determine the winner.

Luck often plays a role in many board games. Steeplechase, which mimics a real horse race, is played out entirely according to the throw of the dice. Other games, such as Pachisi, combine strategy with luck. In fact, Pachisi is an example of a game that can at first be played as one in which chance is more important than strategy. But as you play it again and again and begin to master the game, you will see that it is possible to influence the role of luck by strategically positioning your pieces to out-maneuver and block your opponents. The same opportunity is found in Backgammon. In most of the board games in this book, you can set out to out-wit not only your opponents but chance as well and determine your own fate!

Play It Again is a book for everyone. Whether you want to read the historical information or simply check the rules and play the games, you have the opportunity to discover an extraordinary variety of board games that have been played by children and adults for thousands of years. Easy-to-copy patterns are included for all of the boards and pieces needed to play these games. All you need are paper, cardboard, scissors, pens, pencils, and a ruler to make these simple boards and playing pieces.

Some of the games are very simple to make and easy to learn and can be enjoyed by children under the age of ten. Others are more complicated to learn and master. But the fun of *Play It Again* is that all these games are in one book and you can decide for yourself which ones you want to make and learn to play. Once you have made the boards, started playing the games, and become involved in the strategies necessary to win, you will probably find that the more you play, the more fun they are and that no challenge is too complicated. So, have fun and play it again!

LEXICON.

Some of the most common terms, moves, and rules of gamesmanship used throughout *Play It Again* are explained in this section so that you can get right on with playing the games and testing your luck as well as your skill in out-maneuvering your opponents.

PLAYERS.—The suggested number of players or best combinations of players are listed for each game described in *Play It Again* along with the directions and rules for the games.

PLAYING PIECES or COUNTERS.—Traditionally, stones; seeds; wooden, ivory, and bone pegs; carved wood pyramids; coins; buttons; and marbles are among the many objects that have been used as playing pieces in board games throughout the world. All of the playing-board patterns in *Play It Again* have been designed so that pennies fit easily onto spaces and points. Therefore, we have included instructions on making playing pieces out of pennies in the section "Suggestions for Making Playing Pieces."

DIE (plural, DICE).—A die is usually a small six-sided cube, made of bone, ivory, or plastic, that is marked with one to six dots on its sides. Cubic dice have the advantage of being balanced so that any side should have an equal chance of landing face up. Some of the games in *Play It Again* use a die to determine moves, whereas others use a pair of dice.

The oldest-known dice were probably divining sticks made from twigs. They were rounded on one side and flat on the other, just like more modern carved versions and used in the same way to determine your future. Pyramid-shaped dice, inlaid with ivory and lapis lazulis, were buried in the royal tombs of Ur more than 5,000 years ago. Both four-sided stick dice and cubic ivory and bone dice have also been found in Egyptian tombs.

3

Casting dice to see how they will land has intrigued people for thousands of years. In some countries, such as India, cowrie shells are used to determine the future. Knuckle-bones (from legs of mutton) and divining sticks have also been used as dice in many different countries throughout history by people who believed that the gods would reveal the future to those who understood how to interpret their signs.

Sometimes, in Medieval England, dice were thrown on a dice board. The board was divided into six spaces. A funnel was suspended above the board and the dice were tossed through this cup. Actually, the cast depended not upon the markings of the dice that landed up but upon the value of the space they landed upon.

Otherwise, dice were usually shaken in a wooden cup and tossed out together upon the table. Dice cups are still used today, especially in games like Backgammon, where they are even padded to muffle the sound.

ILLUSTRATION FROM THE SEVENTEENTH CENTURY
OF A DICE-CASTING BOARD AND GAME BOARDS.

DOUBLET or PAIR.—When a pair of dice is thrown and the same number of dots appears on the upper faces of both dice, a "doublet" has been thrown. In most board games, a pair or doublet entitles a player to another throw and turn.

Throwing a doublet may also mean that two playing pieces are joined as a team and moved together as one piece, as in Pachisi.

COCKED DICE.—If one or both of the dice land on top of a piece on the board or are tilted against something, they are "cocked" and should be tossed again.

TEETOTUM.—A teetotum is a four- or six-sided top that is spun with the fingers. The sides are marked with numbers or dots so that the number that lands down when the top stops spinning determines the player's move.

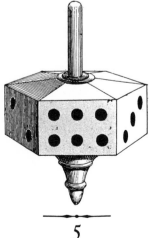

The teetotum probably originated in Germany during the Middle Ages. Originally, teetotums were inscribed with letters and were used to predict the future. Jewish children often play a game with a four-sided top called a *dreidel* that is marked with Hebrew initials. Both dreidels and teetotums can be made of wood, lead, or even fine silver. During the nineteenth century, American children often made teetotums out of cardboard to use to determine the moves in their board games.

THE FIRST MOVE.—Since the first move often gives a player a great advantage in games involving strategy, it is very important to fairly determine who will make the first move. One way is to roll a die or a pair of dice. Each player rolls and the one with the highest throw takes the first turn.

Another method is to flip a coin. One player flips the coin and if the opponent guesses correctly whether heads or tails is up, the opponent begins the game. If the opponent guesses incorrectly, the player makes the first move.

Two players normally alternate turns. If more than two people are playing, turns may be taken either according to the highest numbers thrown or in a clockwise direction around the board.

Further restrictions on the first move, such as special throws or starting squares, are described when they apply to the games in *Play It Again*.

HOME BASE.—The side of the board or space from which a player begins to move his pieces, as in Draughts or Pachisi, is the "home base" of that player. In Pachisi and Ludo, there is also a home space that is really the finishing line, or the final space to be reached by a playing piece in order to win the game.

MOVES.—Playing pieces on the games described in *Play It Again* may be moved in any one of four directions as described in the rules for the individual games. When a piece is moved to an adjacent space or point, it is the square or point next to or adjoining the position of the playing piece.

Forward: Away from a player's home base.
Backward: Back, toward a player's home base.
Sideways: Right or left across the board.
Diagonally: From one corner of a square to another or toward the corner of the board.

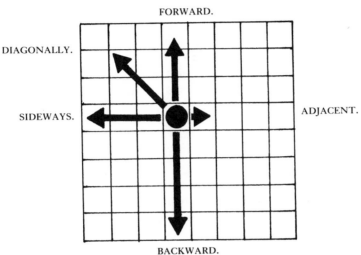

STEP MOVE.—A piece is moved into an adjoining or adjacent space forward, backward, sideways, or diagonally.

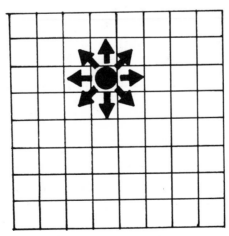

Hop or Jump Move.—A piece is moved over a piece on an adjacent space, onto a vacant space or point directly next to the jumped piece.

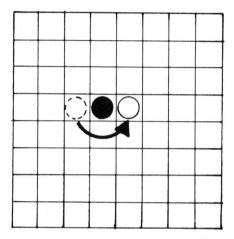

Multiple jumps are allowed in many of the board games in *Play It Again,* as long as the piece making the jump is able to land on a vacant space directly after each jump.

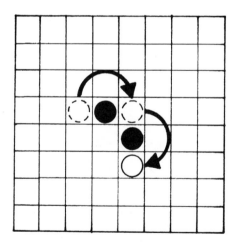

Flank or Out-Flank Move.—When two pieces of one player surround one of the opponent's pieces on both the right and left sides in a straight line, the opponent's piece is out-flanked, and it is usually considered captured and is removed from the board.

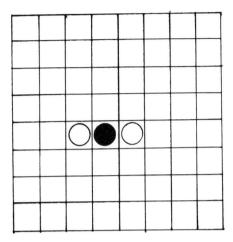

HUFF.—To "huff" a piece is to remove from the board a piece that has been moved wrongly. In some board games, a player's piece may also be huffed by another player if she fails to make a capturing move.

CROWN.—When one playing piece is placed on another one of the same color that has reached the opponent's home base, as in Draughts, the piece is "crowned."

MILL.—Three or more playing pieces placed on adjacent spaces or points in a line form a "mill."

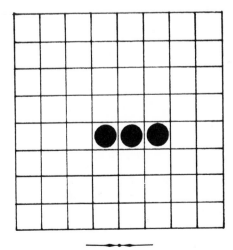

DRAW.—When a board game ends in a "draw," as when neither player is able to make a move, it ends in a tie with neither player winning.

RULES OF GAMESMANSHIP.

In any of the board games in *Play It Again* in which pieces are moved and dice are thrown, there are some rules and penalties that should be remembered. Players should always decide if they are going to observe these rules before they begin to play the games:

Once a player has removed his hand after moving a piece, he may not change the move.

When a player has made an incorrect move, the opponent may insist that the error be corrected if the opponent has not begun her own turn. Some rules state that if a player makes an incorrect move and the opponent catches it, the player automatically forfeits or loses that turn.

If a mistake has been made in setting up the playing pieces on the board, either one of the players may correct it before the first turn is completed.

USEFUL STRATEGIES.

A move that serves several purposes is always better than one that only opens up one option.

Always use the smallest number of pieces necessary to complete a move.

Always decide ahead whether a move will lose or maintain the offensive advantage in a game.

In many games, disconnected pieces are often easier to attack than pieces lined up together.

TOOLS AND SUPPLIES.

The following is a list of suggested tools and supplies that are needed to make the game boards and playing pieces in *Play It Again.* Illustrations and explanations are included to make your job easier in getting together all of the materials that you will need.

Scissors.

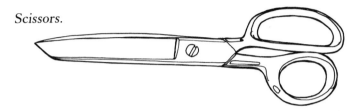

X-acto Knife.

Ruler.

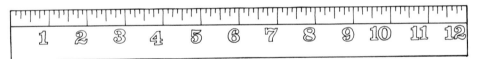

Pencils.

Felt-tip Pens and Markers.

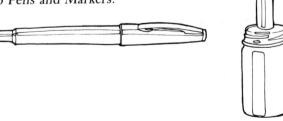

Glue.—Rubber cement or spray adhesive glues will enable you to glue the game-board patterns to the cardboard or posterboard smoothly. White glue may be used to glue heavier-weight cardboard.

Tape.

Paper Fasteners.—Use paper fasteners to assemble the game boards for Pachisi and Ludo and to fasten the spinner pointer to the spinner board.

Tacks.—You may also use tacks to attach the spinner pointer to the spinner board.

Paper.—Plain white paper is best to use for copying most of the boards and playing-piece patterns in this book.

Cardboard and Posterboard.—Medium-weight cardboard can be cut from gift boxes or cardboard packing boxes. Posterboard can be purchased at art-supply stores, stationery stores, college bookstores, and some hobby stores. Heavier cardboard can also be cut from cardboard packing boxes.

SUGGESTIONS FOR COPYING AND ASSEMBLING PLAYING BOARDS.

Game boards and playing pieces have provided an opportunity for craftsmen and artists to create works of art for thousands of years. Boards of inlaid woods, intricately carved ivory, and beautiful colored lithographs, as well as carved and cast playing pieces, are an important part of the tradition and excitement of historic and contemporary board games.

At the same time, many of the board games have been inscribed on stone or drawn on the ground. All over the world and throughout

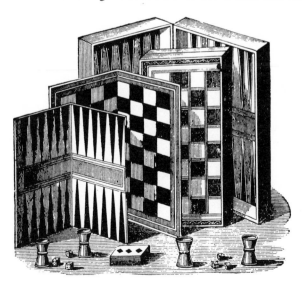

history, people have drawn simple combinations of lines and spaces that make up many of the boards for the games in this book.

All of the board-game patterns in *Play It Again* can easily be traced over with a sheet of lightweight white paper or tracing paper. If you do not want to spend time tracing or copying the patterns, photocopy machines will help you reproduce them quickly and conveniently. After copying the boards and cutting them out, you should assemble and mount them with spray mount or rubber cement onto medium-weight cardboard or posterboard.

You may find it easier to assemble the playing boards by working on a piece of waxed paper so that any extra glue can be easily wiped up.

Some of the playing patterns in *Play It Again* are in one piece and will be very easy to copy and mount. Other patterns have more than one piece and are slightly more complicated to assemble. The more complex patterns are presented in the order in which they should be assembled.

The spaces on boards for such games as the Game of Goose, Snakes and Ladders, and Steeplechase are numbered so that the first number on the second board-pattern piece should follow the last number on the first piece of the pattern. On the Game of Goose board, for example, the second pattern piece connects up with the 3rd space and the 40th space on the first pattern piece; the third pattern piece connects up to the 12th space, and space 46 follows the 45th space on the second pattern piece; and the fourth piece of the pattern connects both the 22nd and 52nd spaces and the 59th and the 32nd spaces on the third pattern piece.

Other playing boards, such as those for the versions of Draughts, Nyout, and Fox and Geese, have more than one identical pattern piece. On the patterns such as these, a flap is included that indicates where to glue the pieces together. Place one pattern piece down, put glue on the flap, and position the second piece on the flap and so on until the complete board is assembled, as shown on page 15.

COLORING THE PLAYING-BOARD PATTERNS.—The boards in *Play It Again* can be left plain or may be colored with felt-tip pens. Pachisi and Ludo boards, for example, are traditionally colored red, green, blue, and yellow. Some of the board patterns have been drawn to look like inlaid wood and could be carefully shaded to give the feeling of a

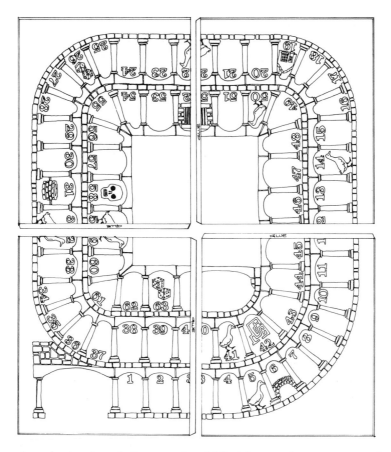

wooden playing board. So, you should feel free to decorate your playing boards in any way that pleases you!

MAKING MORE-ELABORATE PLAYING BOARDS.—All of the board-game patterns included in *Play It Again* can be used to make more-elaborate and carefully crafted game boards. Games using pits, such as Mancala and Wari, can be made out of clay. Press a slab of clay with a rolling pin until it becomes flat. Trim the piece of clay into the shape of a rectangle and make a depression in the clay for each of the pits. Designs can be inscribed into the board before the clay is fired in a kiln. Different glazes will not only add color to the board but will also provide it with a resilient surface.

Games like Pachisi have traditionally been made of cloth so that they could easily be rolled up and carried around. The Pachisi-board pattern included in *Play It Again* can be used as a guide for cutting strips of cloth to make a board. Once the strips are sewn together to form the cross-shaped board, brightly colored yarn or embroidery thread can be used to decorate the board.

Wooden boards provide a particularly interesting challenge for the craftsman. Lightweight plywood provides an excellent surface for making many of the boards in *Play It Again*. Wood stains, varnishes, and paint can be used to decorate the surfaces of the playing boards. Strips of molding or plastic colored tape can be used to finish and frame the edges of the boards.

Lines in the playing surfaces of wooden boards can be made by inscribing them with an awl and then filling in the indentations with paint or colored tapes.

More elaborate wooden boards, such as those for Backgammon and Draughts, may be inlaid with pieces of different types of wood. Holes or spaces can be carved out of solid boards for games played with marbles, such as Solitaire or Chinese Checkers.

DICE, TEETOTUMS, AND SPINNERS.

Since making accurate dice is extremely difficult, we suggest that you either buy a set of dice from a toy, hobby, or dime store or that you use a pair from another game you may already own.

A simple teetotum can be made to use in games that only use one die. Simply copy one of the patterns shown below and glue it onto a

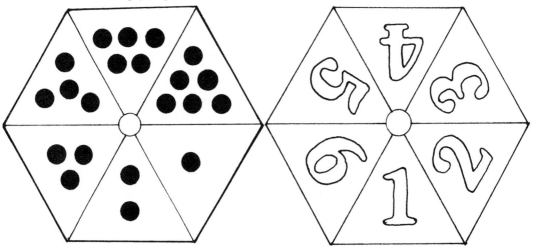

piece of posterboard. Cut it out and then punch a sharpened pencil stub through the center. Spin the teetotum with your fingers by twirling the eraser end of the pencil.

You may also make a simple spinner to be used in games that require only one die. Copy the patterns shown below and glue them onto lightweight cardboard. Cut out the spinner board and pointer. You can attach the pointer to the board with a paper fastener. A tack can also be used to attach the pointer to the spinner board if the board is mounted on a piece of thick cardboard or a piece of wood.

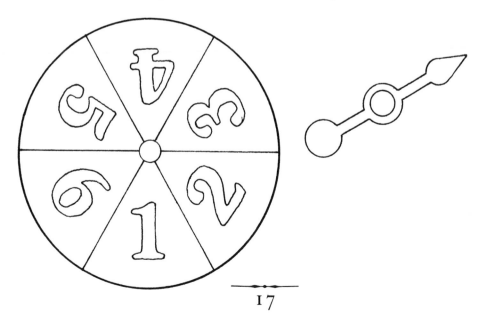

SUGGESTIONS FOR MAKING
PLAYING PIECES.

Throughout history, people have used all sorts of materials and objects as playing pieces for board games. Nearly all of the games in *Play It Again* will require at least two different colors of pieces. You may use such simple objects as pennies, nickels and dimes, buttons, or even seeds to play the games. Pennies and other coins may be painted different colors (spray paint works best) for different players.

You can also place the number of pennies required for each game on pieces of white or black paper. Draw around them, and cut the circles out and glue them onto the pennies. Three-quarter-inch adhesive marker dots, which come in many different colors and may be purchased at most stationery stores, can also be applied to the pennies to make different-colored playing pieces.

Playing-piece patterns are included with each game. All of the patterns are designed so that they can be copied and taped or glued onto a penny or piece of lightweight cardboard or posterboard. Special patterns are included for special pieces: "K" patterns for knights or kings; "Q" patterns for queens; and even horses for the Steeplechase game. Whenever more than two colors of playing pieces are needed, as in Pachisi or Halma, patterns are provided for a black and a white piece and an additional two white pieces that can be colored any color you want.

GAME OF GOOSE

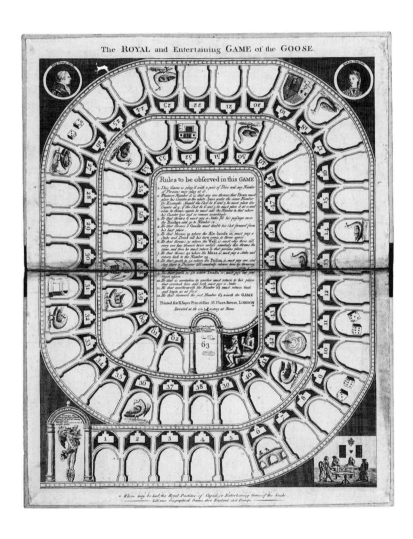

THE GAME OF GOOSE is often called the "Royal Game of Goose" because it is said that the first Goose game (*Giuoco dell'Oca*) was sent by Francesco de Medici of Florence, Italy, to King Phillip II of Spain in the sixteenth century. By 1597, this game of luck had been introduced into England, where it became just as popular as it was on the European continent.

The earliest Goose games consisted of simple journeys and adventures that depended upon chance and the roll of the dice to finish and be the winner. Good luck was rewarded, but bad luck was punished! The early boards were decorated with elaborate spiral courses that often depicted religious, mythological, political, or historical themes. By the eighteenth century, many of these games, such as those based upon Aesop's Fables, were used to teach children moral lessons.

Boards for the Game of Goose are often very dramatic. Different images, such as a death's head or a bridge, representing the trials and rewards of life, make up the 63 squares of the spiral board. Each square of the board is numbered from one to 63, beginning at the farthest outside point of the spiral. As players roll their dice and move their pieces along the squares, they experience sudden changes in fortune

NINETEENTH-CENTURY FRENCH
GAME OF GOOSE BOARD.

REGLE DU JEU DE L'OIE

CHILDREN PLAYING THE GAME OF GOOSE.

involving various penalties and bonus moves. Squares decorated with a Goose appear at regular intervals (5, 14, 22, 32, 41, 50, and 59) that allow the players an extra turn. The first player to complete the course and triumph over bad luck wins the game.

HOW TO PLAY THE GAME OF GOOSE.

NUMBER OF PLAYERS.—At least two.

OBJECTIVE.—To be the first player to reach the 63rd square on the playing board and win the game.

MATERIALS.—Spiral playing board of 63 squares, a set of dice, and a playing piece of a different color for each player.

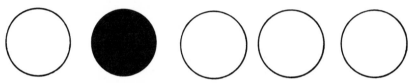

TO BEGIN PLAY.—Each player throws the dice, and the player with the highest number takes the first turn. Players in turn throw the dice and move their pieces the number of squares equal to the sum thrown.

TO PLAY.—Players will come upon good luck and bad luck as they progress along the spiral board. If one player lands on a square occupied by another player's piece, the player who first landed on the square must return to the square just left by the second player.

A player must land exactly on the 63rd square to win. If a higher number is thrown, the player is penalized and must move backwards a number of squares equal to the number of those in excess of 63. If this brings him to a square with a Goose, he must move backwards a number equal to twice the excess number!

REWARDS AND PUNISHMENTS
IN THE GAME OF GOOSE.

Number 6.—BRIDGE.

If a player's piece lands on Number 6, she advances over the Bridge to Number 12.

Number 19.—INN.

A player must remain at the Inn until all the other players have each had two turns.

Number 31.—WELL.

The player must pay a fine by losing two turns.

Number 42.—MAZE.

When a player lands on square Number 42, he must return to square Number 30.

Number 52.—PRISON.

A player landing on this square must remain here until freed by another player landing on the same square.

Number 58.—DEATH'S HEAD.

If a player lands on this square, she is severely punished by having to return to square Number 1 and begin the game all over.

Numbers 26 and 63.— DICE.

When a player lands on square Number 26 or 63, he may throw the dice again in the same turn and take another turn.

Numbers 5, 14, 22, 32, 41, 50, 59.—GOOSE.

When a player lands on a square with a Goose, she gets a second throw of the dice.

23

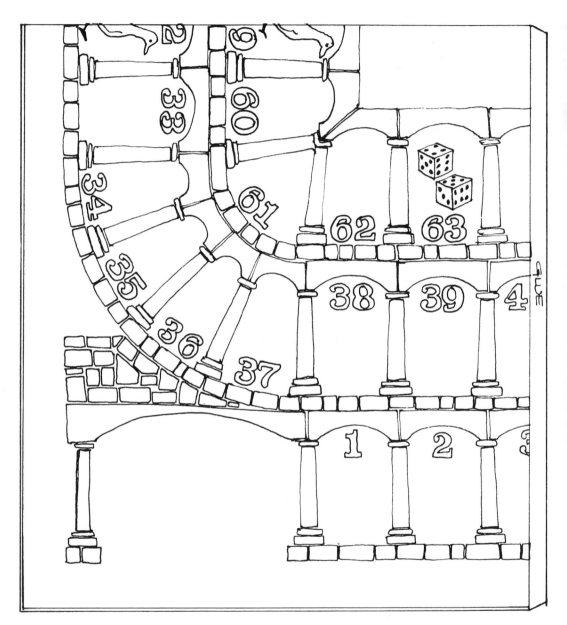

GAME OF GOOSE PLAYING-BOARD PATTERN.—I.

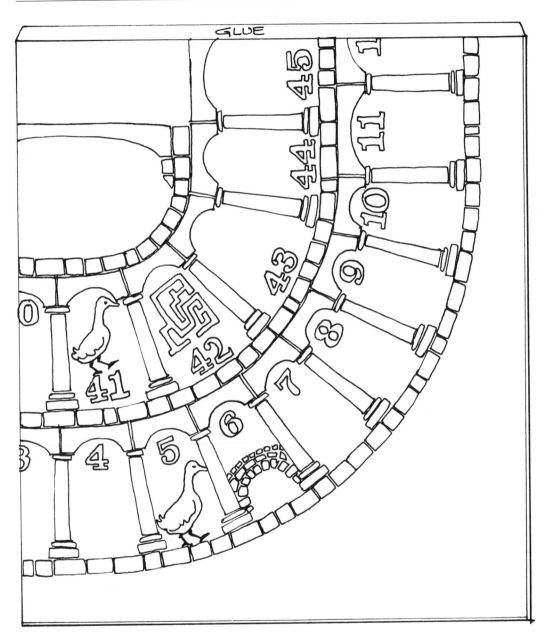

GAME OF GOOSE PLAYING-BOARD PATTERN.—2.

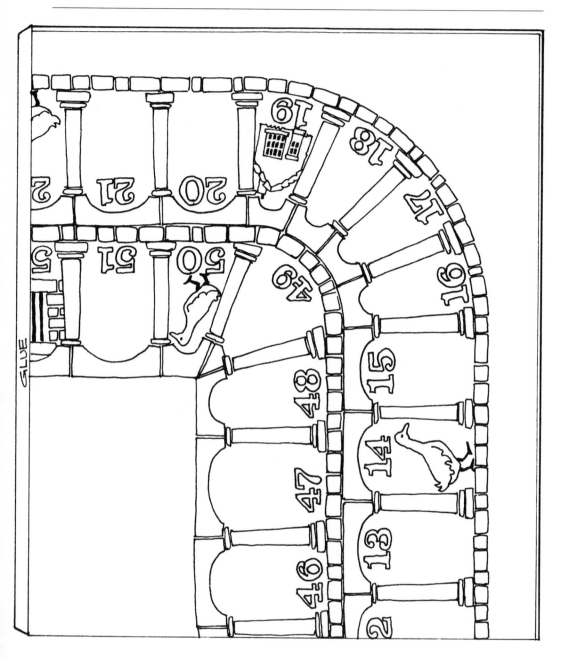

GAME OF GOOSE PLAYING-BOARD PATTERN.—3.

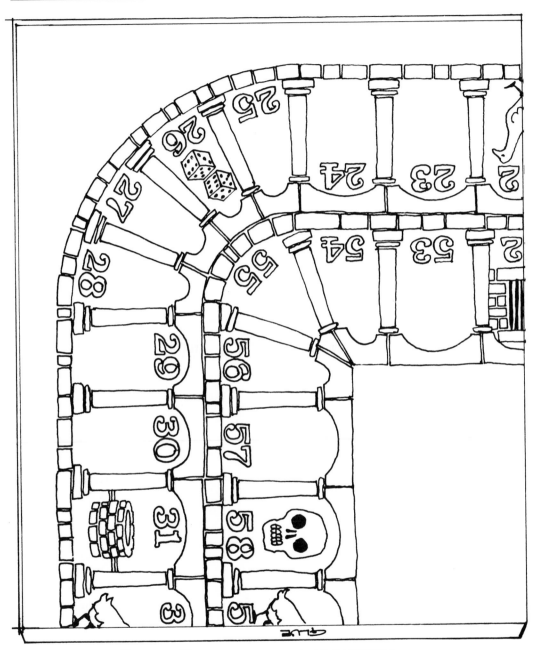

GAME OF GOOSE PLAYING-BOARD PATTERN.—4.

NINE MEN'S MORRIS

SIX MEN'S MORRIS
THREE MEN'S MORRIS
ACHI

N INE MEN'S MORRIS is not only one of the world's most exciting strategy games, but it is also one of its oldest. Boards for the game have been found carved into the roof of the Egyptian temple of Kurna, dating from 1400 B.C., and they are illustrated in fifteenth-century Medieval manuscripts as well.

The board for Nine Men's Morris consists of concentric squares connected with one another by lines. By strategically placing and maneuvering their nine pieces, each player tries to capture or block at least seven of the opponent's pieces.

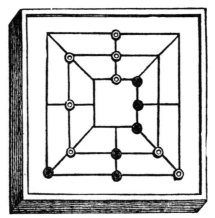

NINE MEN'S MORRIS BOARD.

Nine Men's Morris boards have been scratched on the ground with a stick all over the world. Evidence has been found that the game was played in Bronze-Age Ireland, ancient Troy, and Viking Norway, as well as in the Southwestern United States, where Kere, Tigua, Tewa, and Zuni Indians played versions of the game known as *paritariya*, *picarva*, and *pedreria*. In France, the game was originally called *merelles* and today is known as *jeu de moulin* (Game of Mill), whereas in Germany it has always been called *muhle* (mill).

New versions of Nine Men's Morris are always being invented. For example, several war games, such as "Trencho," inspired by trench fighting, appeared during World War I. In many of these battle games, a Morris board was superimposed upon a map and decorated with battle scenes and military equipment.

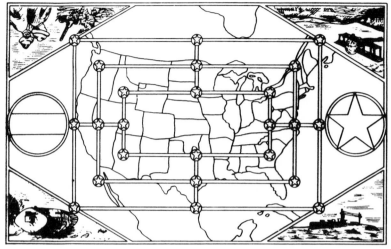

A GAME BOARD PATENTED IN THE
UNITED STATES IN 1918.

HOW TO PLAY
NINE MEN'S MORRIS.

NUMBER OF PLAYERS.—Two.

OBJECTIVE.—To be the first player to reduce the opponent to only two pieces or to block the opponent so that further moves are impossible.

MATERIALS.—A playing board marked with three concentric squares connected with lines. Each player has nine playing pieces of his or her own color.

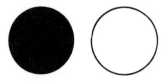

TO BEGIN PLAY.—The game is played on the 24 points of intersection of the lines on the board. The players decide who is to go first and then the first player places one of her pieces on the board at one of the points of intersection. The players continue alternating turns.

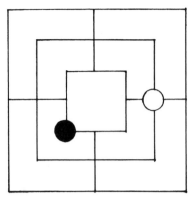

To Play.—The players take turns placing one of their pieces on an empty point on the board wherever two lines intersect, trying to get three of their pieces in a row in order to form a "mill."

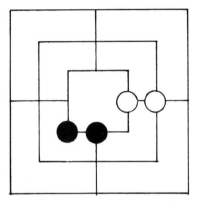

Once a player has formed a mill, he is entitled to "pound" the opponent by removing one of her pieces from the board.

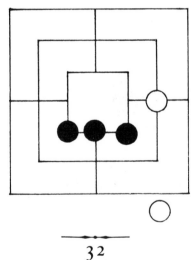

A player may not remove an opponent's piece if it is part of a mill unless there are no other pieces available on the board. Once a piece is removed from the board, it cannot be used again.

When all of the pieces have been laid down (nine turns for each player), the players then attempt to create new mills by maneuvering their pieces. A player may move each of her pieces from its existing

NINE MEN'S MORRIS PLAYING-BOARD PATTERN.

position on one of the points of intersection to any adjacent point that is free. Mills may be broken and re-formed any number of times by moving one of the pieces off the line and then returning it to its former position. Each time a mill is re-formed or a new one is created, a player is entitled to pound his opponent and remove one of her pieces.

The game continues until one player is reduced by successive poundings to only two pieces on the board or until one player's pieces are blocked by the opponent's pieces so that the player is unable to make a move.

SIX MEN'S MORRIS

SIX MEN'S MORRIS is a version of Nine Men's Morris that is played on a board marked with two concentric squares. Each player has six playing pieces of his or her own color to place on the board, one at a time in alternating turns. The purpose of the game is to form a mill and pound the opponent.

As in Nine Men's Morris, once all 12 of the pieces have been placed on the board, the game is continued by the players' moving pieces to adjacent free points in order to form new mills. Both placing the pieces on the board and moving them are equally important in the one-on-one strategy of the game.

When one player has only two pieces left, or cannot move because her pieces are blocked, the game is over.

THREE MEN'S MORRIS

THREE MEN'S MORRIS is played on such a simple board that it looks quite easy. But don't be deceived, for this game can be one of the most fast-paced of all board games! The board is marked with a square divided into four equal squares. Each player has four pieces of his or her own color. Players alternate turns, placing their pieces on points of intersecting lines until one completes a mill and is the winner.

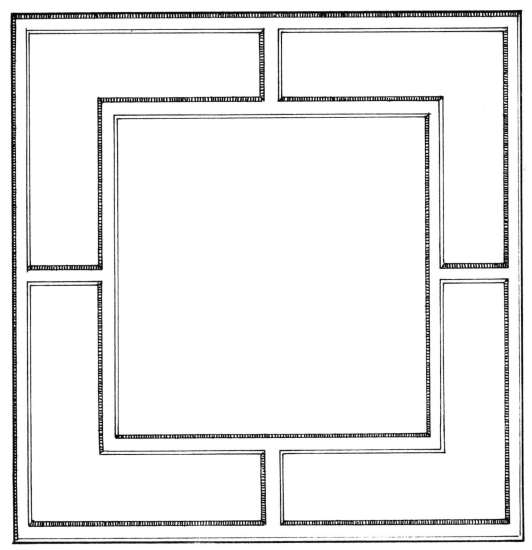

SIX MEN'S MORRIS PLAYING-BOARD PATTERN.

THREE MEN'S MORRIS PLAYING-BOARD PATTERN.

ACHI

ACHI, a Central African variation of Nine Men's Morris, is often played by children on a board drawn in the dirt. Stones are used as playing pieces. With easy-to-learn rules, Achi is played simply and quickly and is another example of why the Morris-type games are some of the most popular board games throughout the world.

DESIGN.

J. J. DONAHUE & J. H. SULLIVAN.
GAME BOARD.

№ 25,349.   Patented Apr. 7, 1896.

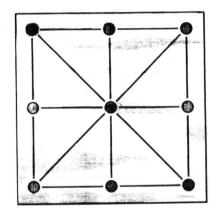

Witnesses.   Inventors
                                        J J Donahue.
                                        J H Sullivan,
                                        By
                                        Southgate & Southgate
                                        Attorneys

Each player is given four pieces of his or her own color to play with. The object of the game is to be the first player to place three pieces in a row, forming a mill, as in Tic-Tac-Toe. Achi begins with both players' placing their pieces on the points of intersection of the lines on the board, in alternating turns.

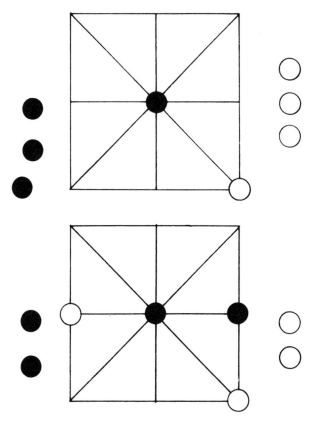

When all eight pieces are on the board, the players may move one piece each turn along the lines to a vacant point of intersection, trying to arrange three pieces in a row, in order to win the game.

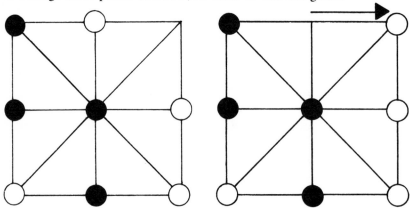

ACHI PLAYING-BOARD PATTERN.

PACHISI

LUDO

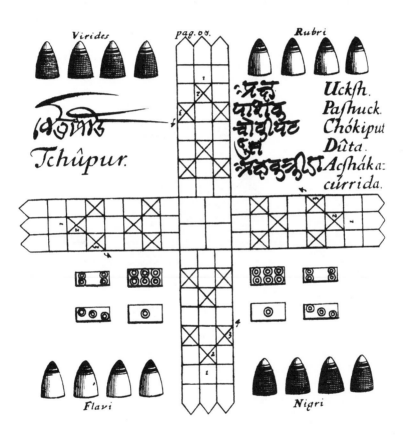

Virides pag. 00. Rubri

Tchûpur.

Ucksh.
Pashuck.
Chókiput
Dûta.
Acshák a:
currida.

Flavi Nigri

41

PACHISI, a game with equal measures of luck and skill, has been played in India for more than 1,200 years. Some Indian rulers liked the game so much that they built giant marble Pachisi boards in their palace courtyards. Akbar the Great, a Mogul Emperor who ruled from 1556–1605, played on a huge board of red and white squares. In the center was an enormous stone platform where Akbar sat. He and his friends actually played the game with young slaves from his harem as playing pieces! Each player had 16 girls, dressed in different colors, who moved along the squares on the board according to the numbers thrown on the cowrie-shells used to play the game.

A GIANT PACHISI BOARD IN AN OLD
INDIAN-PALACE COURTYARD.

The name "Pachisi" comes from the Indian word for twenty-five, which is the highest number that could be thrown on the cowrie-shell dice. Today, Pachisi is also played in Indian homes and cafes, usually on boards made of decorated cloth that can be rolled up and carried about.

Eventually, Pachisi became known in Europe, where it was mentioned as early as 1694 by the Englishman Thomas Hyde in his famous book *De Ludis Orientalibus* (Games of the Orient), which is one of the first books ever written about games.

By the late 1800s, Pachisi had also become a very popular game in the United States, where it was called Pachisi, Parchesi, Parcheesi, or even Chessindia. All of these variations of Pachisi combine judgment and skill as the players try to make the best possible moves. In this way, Pachisi is a lot like the game of Backgammon.

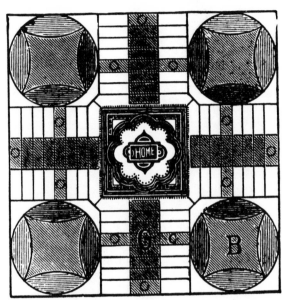

A 1908 SEARS, ROEBUCK & CO. CATALOGUE
ADVERTISEMENT FOR PACHISI.

HOW TO PLAY PACHISI.

NUMBER OF PLAYERS.—Two people can play, or four players can compete in teams of two.

OBJECTIVE.—Each player tries to move his or her four playing pieces around the board and back into the central starting space before their opponents.

MATERIALS.—A cross-shaped playing board divided into 96 smaller squares and a central space called the *charikoni*, or home space. Twelve of the smaller squares are designated as safe resting spaces. In the English versions of Pachisi, these spaces were often called castles.

Playing pieces are free from capture here and if a castle is occupied, a partner's piece may also rest here, but it is off limits to an opponent's piece.

Each player has four playing pieces of his or her own color.

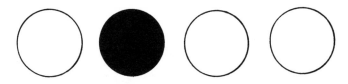

A die is needed to play the game, or you can use six pennies in place of the cowrie-shells that are traditionally used as dice. The pennies are scored as follows:

2 heads up ———	2
3 heads up ———	3
4 heads up ———	4
5 heads up ———	5
6 heads up ———	6 and another throw
1 head up ———	10 and another throw
0 heads up ———	25 and another throw

TO BEGIN PLAY.—Each player places his or her four pieces in the center of the board. If four people are playing, those sitting opposite each other are partners. Each player throws the six pennies (or die cowrie-shells, if you have them) to determine who begins the game. The player with the highest throw throws again and begins. Turns are then taken by the players, counterclockwise around the board.

Each piece is moved from the *charikoni* down the center of the player's side of the cross and then around the board, counterclockwise, and back up the center of his or her own side to the *charikoni*. Once a piece has made it around the board and into the *charikoni*, it should be removed from the board so that it will not be mistaken for captured pieces or pieces that haven't yet left the *charikoni*.

A player's first piece may enter the board on any throw, but the other three pieces (or the first piece if it has been captured and has to repeat the trip) can only enter on a throw of 6, 10, or 25. Pieces can only reenter the *charikoni* after completing their trip around the board, on an exact throw.

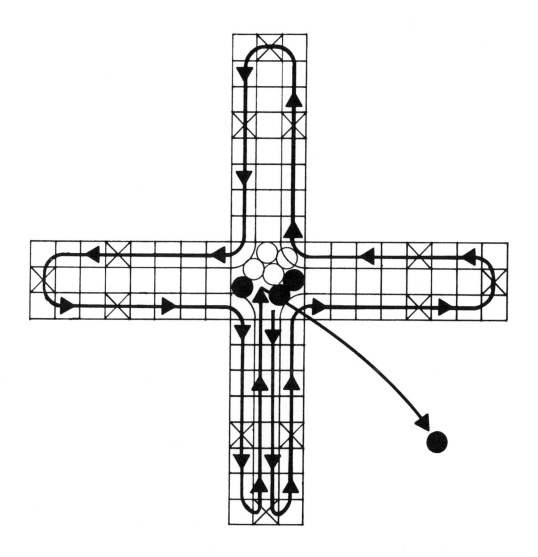

To Play.—Each player moves a piece the number of spaces indicated by the throw of the pennies or cowrie-shells. If a player gets to throw again in the same turn (by throwing 0, 1, or 6 heads up), the second throw may be used to move a different piece. A single throw may not be split between more than one piece. After having had at least one turn, a player may refuse to throw or to move in order to prevent being captured or to help his partner.

As the pieces are moved around the board, they may be captured unless they are on a castle square. These are marked with an *x*. A player captures an opponent's piece by landing on the same square occupied by the opponent. The opponent's piece is removed from the square and placed in the *charikoni*, and it must re-enter the board again. The player making the capture gets another turn. When a piece makes its way back to the center row of its own arm of the cross, it is safe and may not be captured.

A player, or partners, may double pieces to create a blockade by moving two pieces to the same square. An opponent or the same player cannot move a single piece past this blockade, and the blockade can only be captured by two or more of the opponent's pieces landing on the blockade at once. If the blockade is on a castle square, it may not be captured. Two or more pieces making up a blockade may be moved around the board together on a single throw.

When a player reaches her own arm of the cross, she may decide to continue on a second trip around the board instead of moving up the center of the *charikoni* in order to help out her partner. The player or partners who manage to move all of their pieces around the board and back into the *charikoni* first win the game.

NOTE ON ASSEMBLING THE
PACHISI PLAYING BOARD.

The Pachisi playing board may be assembled in two ways: You may copy the four pattern pieces and cut them out and mount them on a piece of posterboard so that the four center rings match up, one on top of the other; or, you may copy the pieces and mount them and cut them out and then fasten them together by punching a paper fastener or tack through the center rings of each piece, one after another, so that all four pieces are connected at the center.

PACHISI PLAYING-BOARD PATTERNS.—1 and 2.

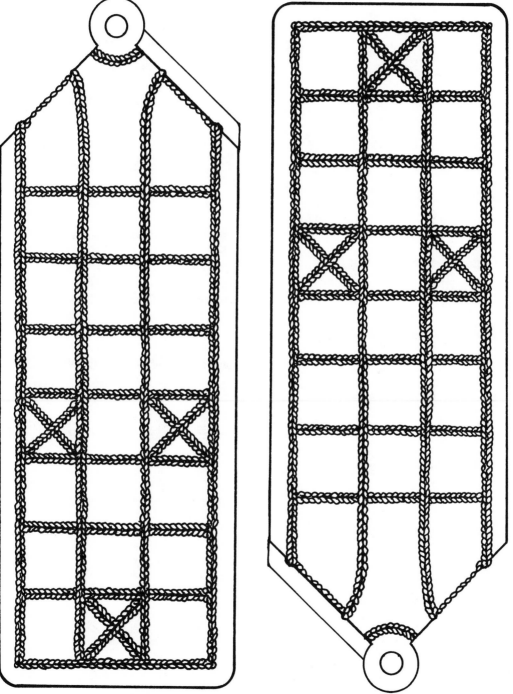

PACHISI PLAYING-BOARD PATTERNS.—3 and 4.

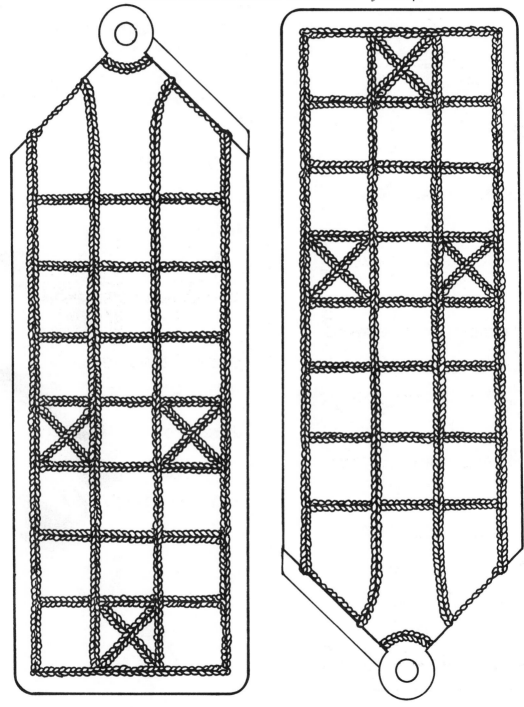

LUDO

LUDO, a much simpler version of Pachisi for children, was popular in England and the United States at the end of the nineteenth century. It is played with one die instead of six pennies or cowrie shells.

HOW TO PLAY LUDO.

NUMBER OF PLAYERS.—Two, three, or four.

OBJECTIVE.—To be the first player to move all four of his pieces safely into his home space.

MATERIALS.—A square board with four arms of a cross leading to the central home space. In each corner of the board are the home bases for each player's four pieces, all of a different color from their opponent's pieces. Traditionally, the Ludo board and playing pieces are colored red, blue, green, and yellow. There are no safe squares on the board as in Pachisi, but once a player's pieces have reached the central row of the arm leading to her home space, they are safe from capture. A die is used to determine the moves.

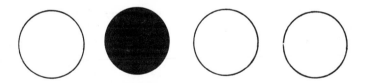

TO BEGIN PLAY.—Each player chooses which color of home base and pieces he or she wants to play with, and then the die is thrown to see who gets the highest number and will take the first turn. The pieces are moved around the board from each player's starting point in a clockwise direction, as shown at the top of page 50.

Each player must roll a 6 in order to place a piece on the starting space. Throughout the game, whenever a player rolls a 6, he is allowed another throw of the die. The number thrown on the die cannot be divided between two or more pieces, unless a player rolls a 6, when a different piece may be moved for the second throw.

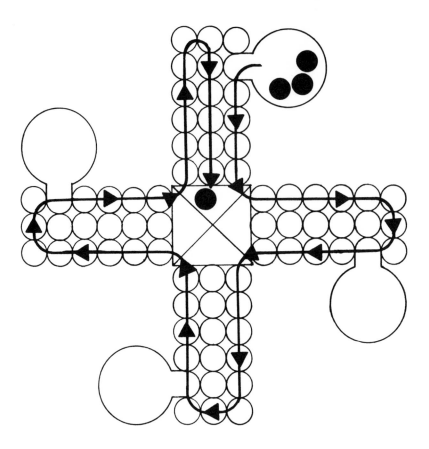

To Play.—If a player's piece lands on a space already occupied by an opponent's piece, the opponent's piece is captured and sent back to its home base, where it can only re-enter the board when a 6 is thrown on the die.

Once a piece has entered the last five spaces before its home space, it is safe from capture by an opponent's pieces.

A piece may be moved into the home space only when the exact number needed is thrown on the die. The game is over when one player has all four of her pieces moved into her home space.

NOTE ON ASSEMBLING THE LUDO PLAYING BOARD.

The Ludo playing board is assembled in the same way as the Pachisi board. After copying, mounting, and cutting out the four separate pieces of the board, connect all four through their centers with a paper fastener or a tack.

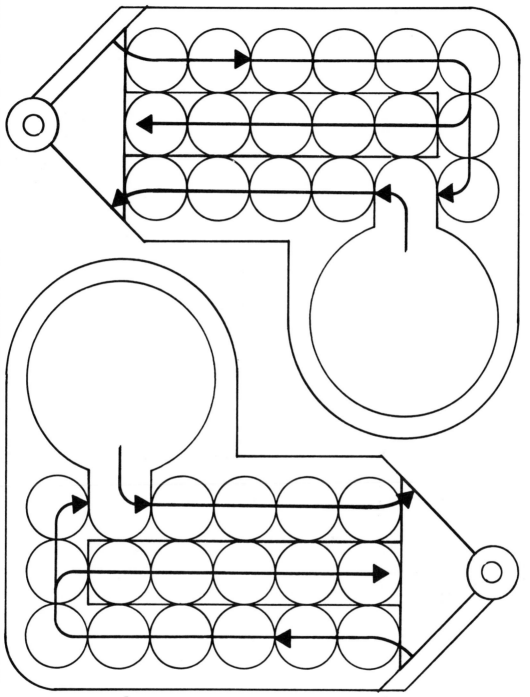

LUDO PLAYING-BOARD PATTERNS.—1 and 2.

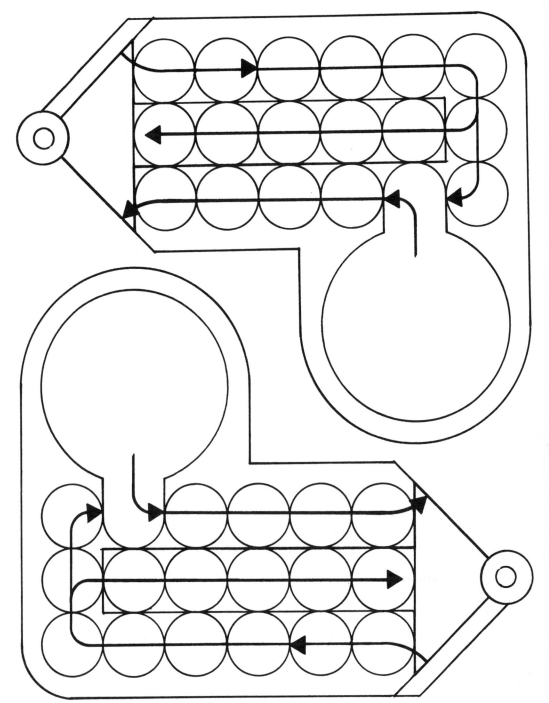

LUDO PLAYING-BOARD PATTERNS.—3 and 4.

SNAKES AND LADDERS

Snakes and ladders has been a favorite race game with children in England and America for nearly one hundred years. Even though it is a simple game of chance, it becomes exciting when good luck is dramatically rewarded and bad luck is disastrously punished! Imagine landing on the head of a snake on square 97 and having to slip all the way back down the snake to square 8! But you can also have the good luck to land on square 19 and climb up the ladder all the way to square 91.

As you can see, winning in race games such as Snakes and Ladders is entirely dependent upon the luck of your throw of the die, so all players are really equals.

Snakes and Ladders is probably based upon a very old Indian game called *moksha-patamu*, in which good and evil exist side by side. The game teaches that virtuous acts, which are represented by the ladders, will shorten the journey across the board, just as the Hindus believe that these acts aid the soul's journey to perfection in real life. Evil deeds and bad luck are represented by the snakes. Just as bad luck or an evil deed will set you back in real life, landing on a snake means that your playing piece must be moved back down the snake's body to the square at its tail.

HOW TO PLAY SNAKES AND LADDERS.

NUMBER OF PLAYERS.—Any number.

OBJECTIVE.—To be the first player to escape as many of the evil snakes as possible and safely reach the 100th square at the end of the board.

MATERIALS.—A playing board consisting of 100 squares. Varying numbers of snakes and ladders, representing good and bad luck, are depicted on the board. The heads of the snakes are always at a higher-numbered square than their tails. Each player uses a playing piece of a different color from the opponent's piece. Moves are determined by the throw of one die.

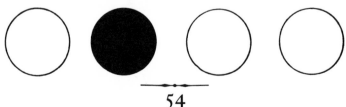

To Begin Play.—As in many other race games, there are different rules for playing Snakes and Ladders. The following rules are only one way to play the game.

Each player rolls the die to see who goes first. The player with the highest roll takes the first turn. The other players take their turns depending upon the number they rolled.

Each player throws the die and moves his or her piece the number of squares indicated by the throw. However, a player must throw a 6 in order to enter a piece on the number one square on the board. That player then gets to throw again and move the piece the number rolled. Throughout the game, whenever a player throws a 6, a second throw is awarded that player.

To Play.—If a player's piece lands on a square already occupied by an opponent's piece, the opponent's piece is knocked back to the number one square.

Whenever a piece lands on a square marked with the bottom of a ladder, the piece is automatically moved up the ladder to the square at the top.

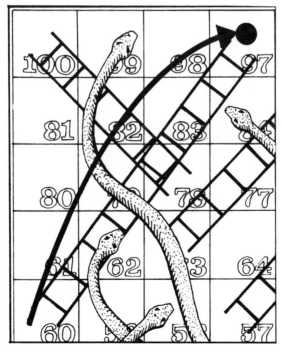

If the player's piece lands on a square marked with a snake's head, the piece must be moved all the way down the snake's body to the square at its tail.

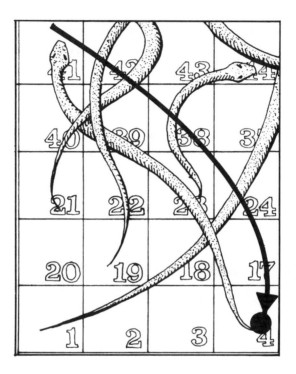

The game is over when one of the player's pieces lands exactly on the 100th square, or the "home" space. If a player's throw is higher than the number needed to land on the home square, then he is penalized and his piece must be moved forward to the 100th square and then back the number of moves remaining in the throw. For example, if a player's piece is on the 98th square, then a 2 throw is required to win the game. But if the player rolls a 3, the piece must be moved forward two squares to the 100th square and then back one square to the 99th square.

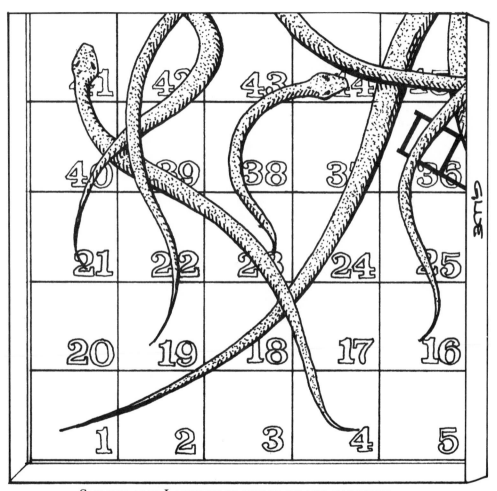

SNAKES AND LADDERS PLAYING-BOARD PATTERN.—I.

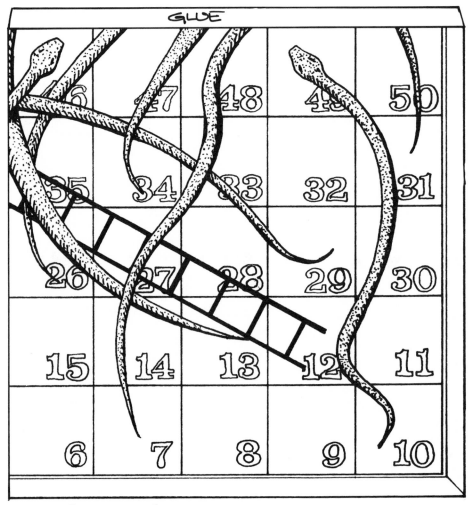

SNAKES AND LADDERS PLAYING-BOARD PATTERN.—2.

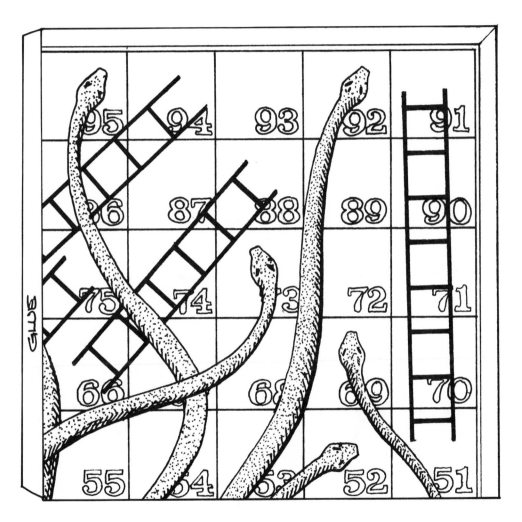

SNAKES AND LADDERS PLAYING-BOARD PATTERN.—3.

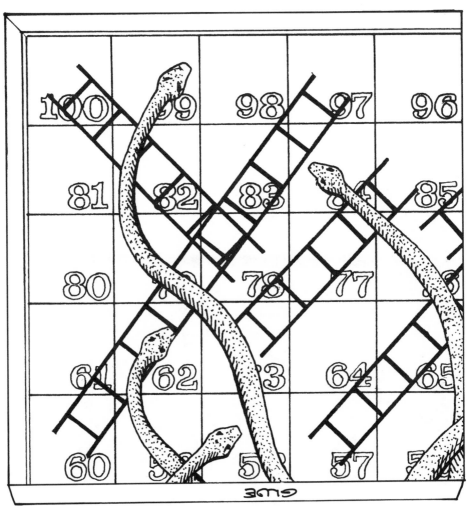

SNAKES AND LADDERS PLAYING-BOARD PATTERN.—4.

ALQUERQUE

FANORONA
FIGHTING SERPENTS
PERALIKATUMA

ALQUERQUE is among the oldest of all board games. Examples of the game have been found dating from 1400 B.C., carved into the roof of the temple of Kurna in Egypt. During the Middle Ages, Alquerque was introduced by the Moors into Spain. Called *el-quirkat* in Arabic, the game and its rules are mentioned in the tenth-century Arabic work *Kitab-al Aghami*. Several different versions of the game also were included in the *Libro de Juegos* (Book of Games) of Alfonso X (A.D. 1251–1282), King of Castile.

Alquerque was brought to the New World by the Spanish and became popular among the Kere and Hopi Indians in the southwestern part of the United States, where it is known as *aiyawatstani* or *tuknanavuhpi*.

Twelve-man Alquerque ("Alquerque de Doce") has probably always been the most popular version of the game. In many respects, the game is similar to Checkers and Chess. It is played on a square board containing 16 smaller squares, each of which is divided by a diagonal line. Each player attempts to jump and capture his or her opponent's pieces. The game remains popular in Spain today.

HOW TO PLAY ALQUERQUE.

NUMBER OF PLAYERS.—Two.

OBJECTIVE.—To capture all of the opponent's pieces.

MATERIALS.—A square playing board divided into 16 smaller squares and 24 playing pieces, 12 of one color for one player and 12 of another color for the second player.

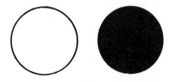

TO BEGIN PLAY.—Place each player's pieces on the board as shown at the top of page 63 and determine who is to take the first move.

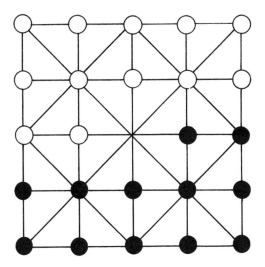

To PLAY.—The game is played by one's moving a piece from its original place on the board to an empty place adjacent to it.

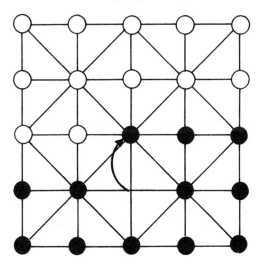

When a player's piece meets an opponent's piece, it may jump over it if the space beyond the piece is vacant. The opponent's piece is then captured and removed from the board for the remainder of the game.

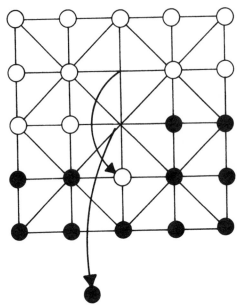

Multiple jumps are allowed in a single move and can include a change in direction.

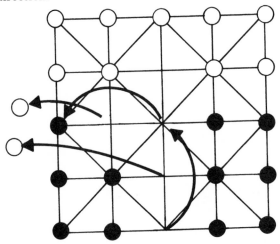

When one player has the opportunity to jump an opponent's piece and does not jump it, her piece is removed from the board and considered captured by the opponent.

A player can win the game of Alquerque by capturing all of his opponent's pieces or by blocking them so that the opponent cannot move. If neither player can move, then the game ends in a draw.

ALQUERQUE PLAYING-BOARD PATTERN.—I.

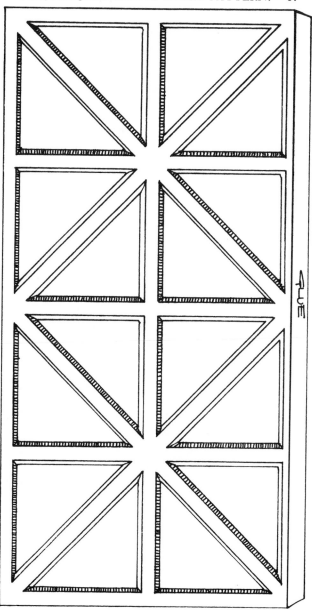

Alquerque Playing-Board Pattern:—2.

FANORONA

FANORONA is an Alquerque game from Madagascar (now the Malagasy Republic) that is said to have magical powers that enable it to predict the future. Invented during the seventeenth century, the game was played on a double Alquerque board inscribed on flat stones or drawn on the ground. Captures in Fanorona are not made by jumping over an opponent's piece as in most of the other versions of Alquerque. Instead, a whole row of the opponent's pieces can be captured by simply maneuvering one of your own pieces next to their row of pieces! This unique capturing move makes Fanorona a fascinating challenge to anyone who has mastered Alquerque.

It was during the storming of the capital of Madagascar by the French in 1895 that the game was supposedly played by the Queen of Madagascar and her advisors, who believed that the outcome of the game would predict who would win the forthcoming battle.

HOW TO PLAY
FANORONA.

NUMBER OF PLAYERS.—Two.

OBJECTIVE.—To capture all of the opponent's pieces.

MATERIALS.—A double Alquerque playing board and 22 playing pieces. Each player uses a different color.

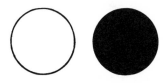

TO BEGIN PLAY.—Place each player's pieces on the board as shown at the top of page 68. One space is left vacant in the center of the board.

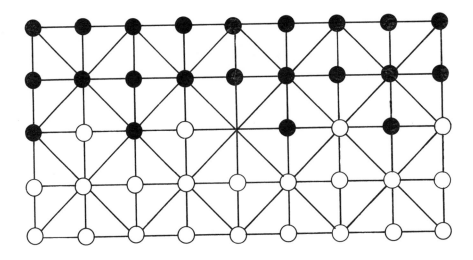

Decide which player will play with the white pieces. That player takes the first turn. Playing pieces may be moved along the lines—diagonally, forward, backwards, or sideways—to a vacant intersection, as shown below.

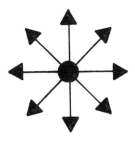

If a player moves a piece next to an opponent's piece without a vacant point in between, then all the opponent's pieces that extend in an unbroken line from that player's piece *in the direction of the attack* are captured and removed from the board.

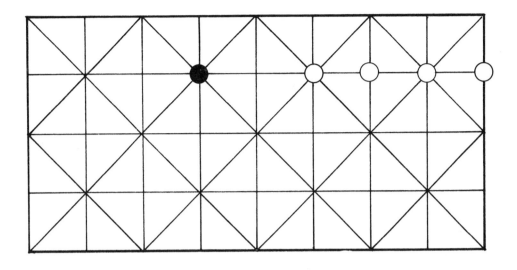

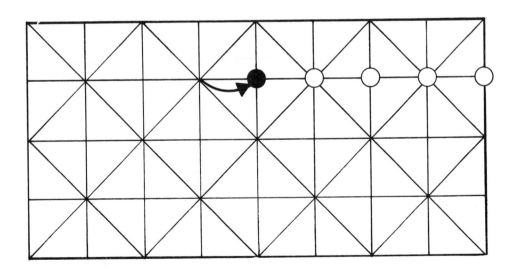

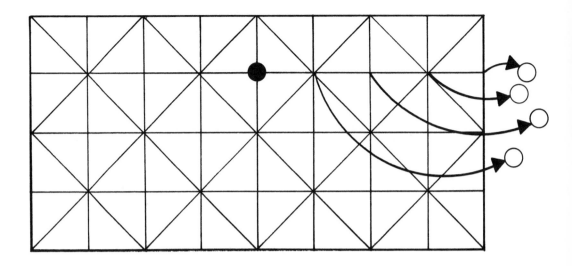

If the line of the opponent's pieces is broken by a vacant point or by one of the player's own pieces, then the opponent's pieces are captured up to that point or piece only, as shown below and opposite.

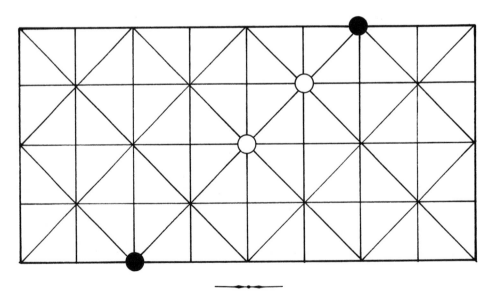

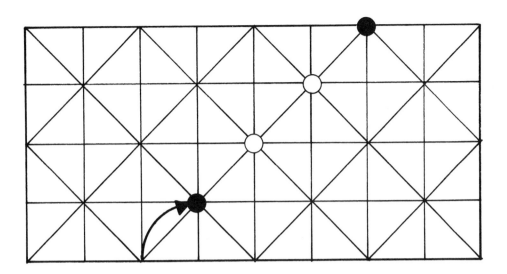

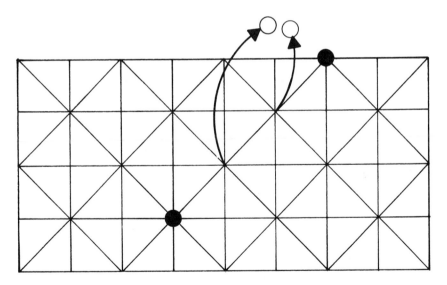

All three of these types of captures are called capture by "approach." Captures may also be made by "withdrawal." If a player moves a piece *away* from a line of the opponent's pieces, then the opponent's pieces in the line of the withdrawal move are captured and removed from the board.

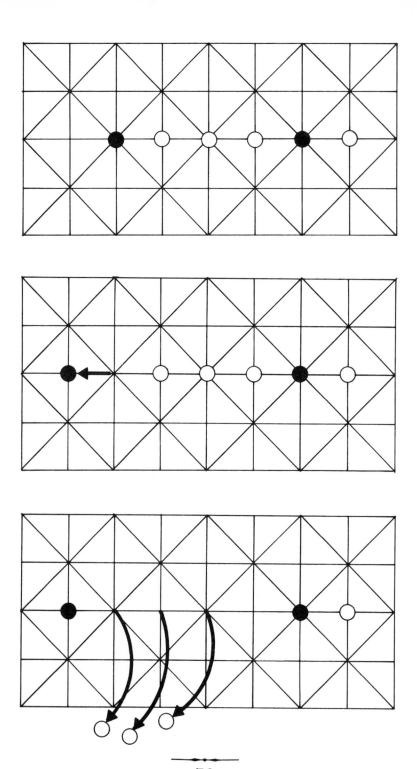

If a player's move threatens two or more rows of the opponent's pieces, the player may decide which row to capture. The player is not required to choose the longest row for capture.

To Play.—The first player is allowed only one move. From then on, each player may continue taking moves until it is no longer possible to capture any of the opponent's pieces. But each move must be along a different line on the board, so that even if the same piece is being moved, it must be moved in different directions.

FANORONA PLAYING-BOARD PATTERN.—I.

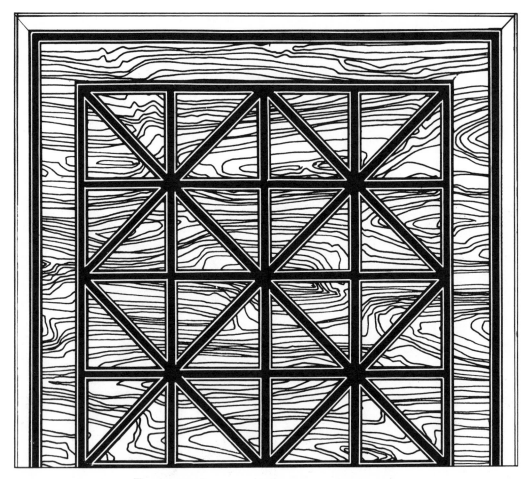

FANORONA PLAYING-BOARD PATTERN.—2.

FIGHTING SERPENTS

FIGHTING SERPENTS is an Alquerque-type game invented by the Zuni Indians of New Mexico. Called *kolowis awithlaknannai*, after the mythical serpent the *kolowisi*, the game tests your ability to out-maneuver your opponent within the tight confines of a narrow board crisscrossed with lines and to capture all of her pieces. The game appears to be based on a quadruple version of Alquerque that was introduced into Mexico by the Spanish Conquistadors in the sixteenth century. The Zuni version of the game is often inscribed on long oval stone slabs or even into the clay roofs of houses.

HOW TO PLAY FIGHTING SERPENTS.

NUMBER OF PLAYERS.—Two.

OBJECTIVE.—To be the first player to capture all of the opponent's playing pieces.

MATERIALS.—A narrow playing board crisscrossed with lines, and 46 playing pieces, 23 for one player and 23 of a different color for the other player.

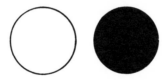

TO BEGIN PLAY.—Place each player's pieces on the board as illustrated below so that only three spaces are left vacant. Decide who will take the first turn.

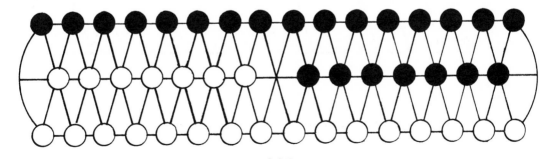

To Play.—The first player moves one of his pieces along the lines to one of the three vacant spaces on the board.

A player must capture an opponent's piece whenever possible. This is done by jumping over one of the opponent's pieces into an empty space next to it. Pieces are removed from the board when they are captured.

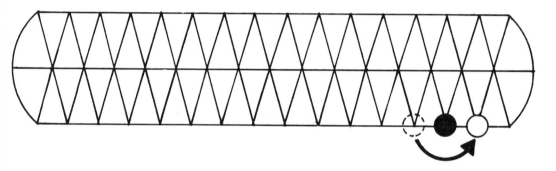

Multiple jumps are allowed and can involve a change in direction, but jumping must be in a straight line. Going around the end of the board is not allowed, as it requires moving in a curved line.

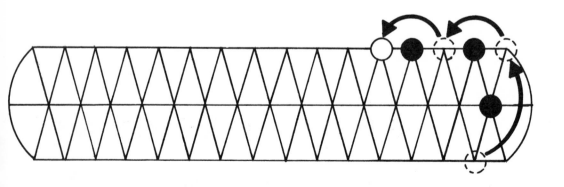

The game ends when all of one player's pieces have been captured.

GLUE

FIGHTING SERPENTS PLAYING-BOARD PATTERN.—1.

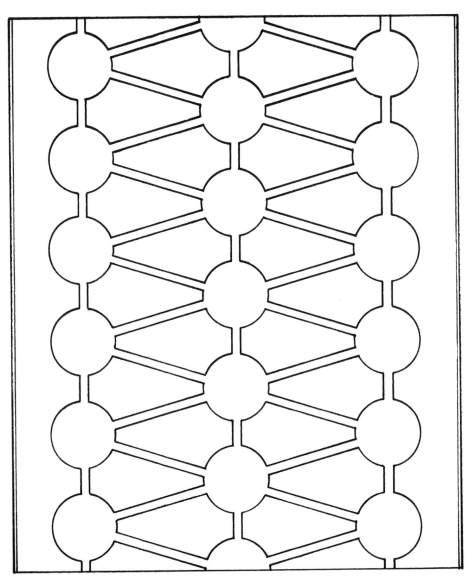

FIGHTING SERPENTS PLAYING-BOARD PATTERN.—2.

FIGHTING SERPENTS PLAYING-BOARD PATTERN.—3.

PERALIKATUMA

PERALIKATUMA is an interesting variation of Alquerque that is played in Ceylon. The rules and strategies are the same as in Alquerque, but the board is quite different. Each player has 23 pieces instead of 12. They are placed on the board as illustrated below.

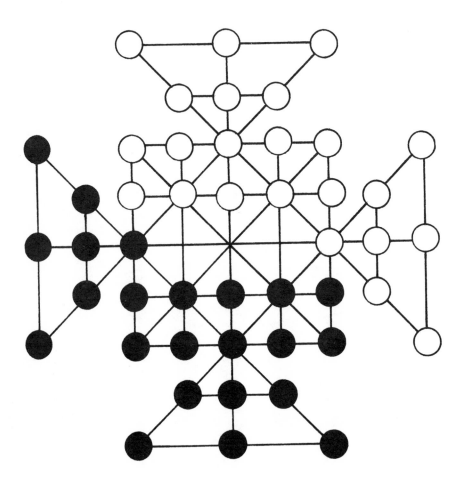

PERALIKATUMA PLAYING-BOARD PATTERN.—I.

PERALIKATUMA PLAYING-BOARD PATTERN.—2.

PERALIKATUMA PLAYING-BOARD PATTERN.—3.

PERALIKATUMA PLAYING-BOARD PATTERN.—4.

SOLITAIRE

THE CROSS

SOLITAIRE is said to have been invented by a French aristocrat to help him pass the time while he was imprisoned in solitary confinement in the Bastille. Played by only one person, Solitaire is a fast-paced game that tests your ability to plot the strategy of each successive move.

Introduced into England at the end of the 1700s, Solitaire continued to be very popular into the Victorian period. In Germany, the game was known as the "hermit's game." It is usually played on a square wooden or plastic board having 33 holes that hold a set of pegs or marbles. More-elaborate boards, including the traditional octagonal French versions with 37 holes, were often made of carved ivory or inlaid woods with ivory or bone pegs.

In the most popular version of Solitaire, the pieces are arranged so that the center hole is vacant. The objective is to clear the board of all but one of the pieces by jumping, horizontally or vertically, over an adjacent piece and removing it from the board. Even though Solitaire is easy to learn, it presents you with an ongoing challenge to master and has become an especially popular board game in recent years.

HOW TO PLAY SOLITAIRE.

NUMBER OF PLAYERS.—One.

OBJECTIVE.—To remove as many pieces as you can from the playing board. The real challenge of Solitaire is to be able to remove all but one piece from the board.

MATERIALS.—A playing board with 33 holes and 32 playing pieces.

TO BEGIN PLAY.—Place a piece over each of the holes in the board, except for the center hole, which is marked with a star.

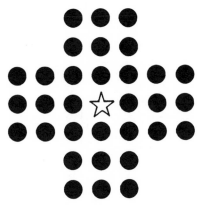

To Play.—Each piece can be moved by jumping backward, forward, or sideways, but not diagonally. When a piece is jumped over by another, it is removed from the board.

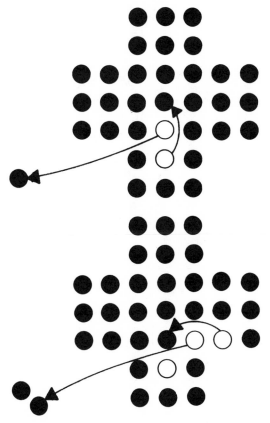

If the game is played correctly, it should end with the last piece left in the center hole marked with the star.

SOLITAIRE PLAYING-BOARD PATTERN.—1.

SOLITAIRE PLAYING-BOARD PATTERN.—2.

THE CROSS

THE CROSS is a variation of Solitaire in which nine pieces are used, positioned on the board as shown below.

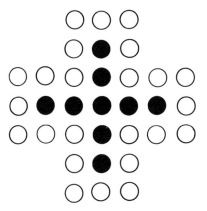

The object of the game is to remove eight of the nine pieces from the board, leaving only one piece left in the center.

You can devise your own versions of Solitaire by setting up new patterns of pieces and attempting to play the game so that only one piece remains at the center of the board.

HALMA

CHINESE CHECKERS

Halma, a battle game in which your only weapon is your ability to plan ahead, was an extremely popular board game invented during the second half of the nineteenth century. Its name is derived from a Greek word meaning "to jump." Played by both children and adults, Halma has the advantage of combining very simple rules that can be learned in a few minutes with the strategic possibilities of moves found in Checkers and Chess.

In the game, each player tries to block, out-maneuver, and outwit his or her opponents and capture the opponent's side of the board by occupying it with all of his or her own pieces. An early advertisement for Halma claimed:

> It has, as a game, the advantage which Dr. Holmes attributes to rowing, as an athletic exercise—you can put into it just as much or as little strength as you choose. Children of eight or ten like it, and the most intellectual people of my acquaintance are delighted with it.

In the United States, Halma was published by the Milton Bradley Company until 1889, when the Halma Company took over its production and sale.

HOW TO PLAY HALMA.

NUMBER OF PLAYERS.—Two, three, or four. The game is best played with either two or four players, each player playing for him- or herself. Four players can also play as partners, but three players must play separately, although in such a case a balanced game is difficult.

OBJECTIVE.—To move all of one's own pieces into the "yard" diagonally across the board from one's starting position. The first player or pair of players to achieve this objective wins the game.

MATERIALS.—A square board divided into 256 squares, 16 by 16. Each corner of the board is separated by a line into a "yard" of 13 squares. Two of the yards, diagonally opposite each other, contain an additional six squares, marked off by another line. These two yards with 19 squares are used when two players play the game. When three or four players play, only the original 13 squares in each yard are used.

Four sets of playing pieces, each set a different color, are used for the game. Two sets must have 19 pieces, whereas the other two sets need only 13 pieces.

To BEGIN PLAY.—In order to play Halma with two players, place 19 pieces in two yards opposite one another, as shown below.

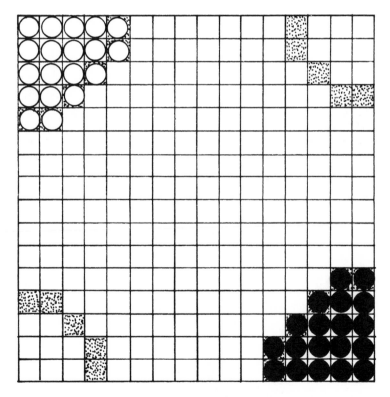

When the game is played by three or four players, 13 pieces are placed on the board, as shown at the top of page 94.

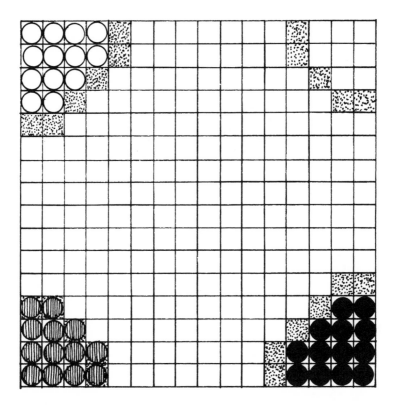

Decide which player will move first. Only one piece may be moved at each turn. Players continue taking turns counterclockwise around the board.

To Play.—The basic move for Halma is to move one piece one space in any direction.

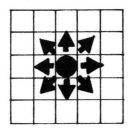

94

Jumping moves are also allowed. A player may jump one piece over an opponent's piece or over one's own piece. Jumps may also be made in any direction, as long as there is a vacant square to land on after each jump. Pieces are not removed from the board when they have been jumped. A player may not combine the basic move or "step" with a jump or "hop" move in the same turn.

The most effective stategy for Halma is to set up a "chain" of pieces across the board that can rapidly be jumped with one's piece, as in Checkers or Draughts.

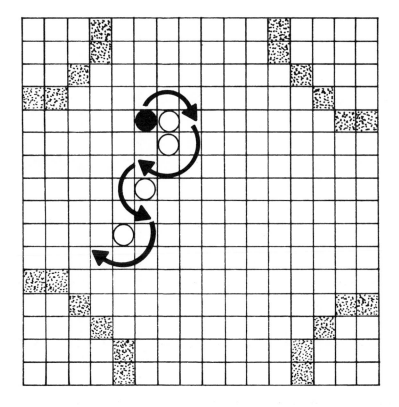

Blocking the opponent's ability to move and jump is also an important element in successfully playing the game of Halma.

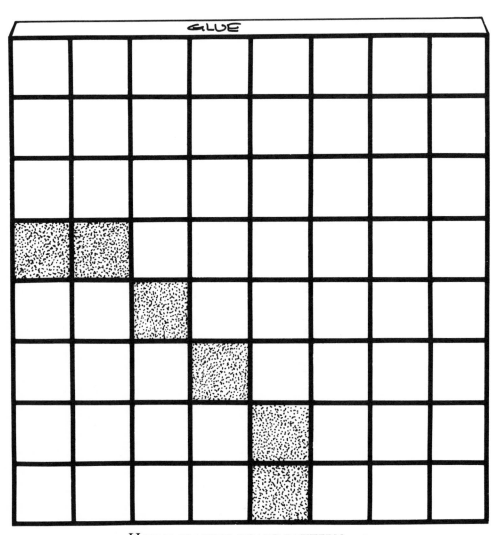

HALMA PLAYING-BOARD PATTERN.—I.

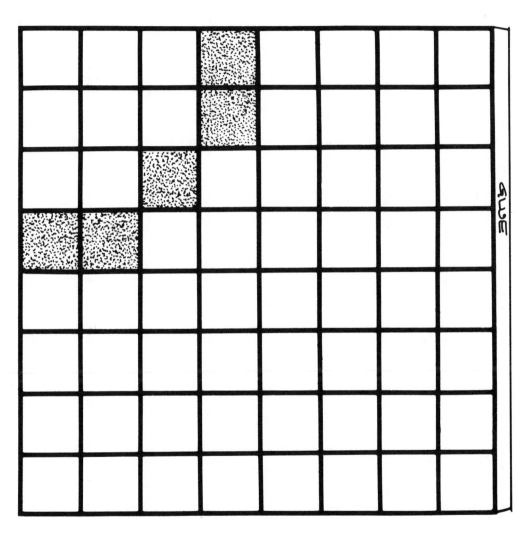

HALMA PLAYING-BOARD PATTERN.—2.

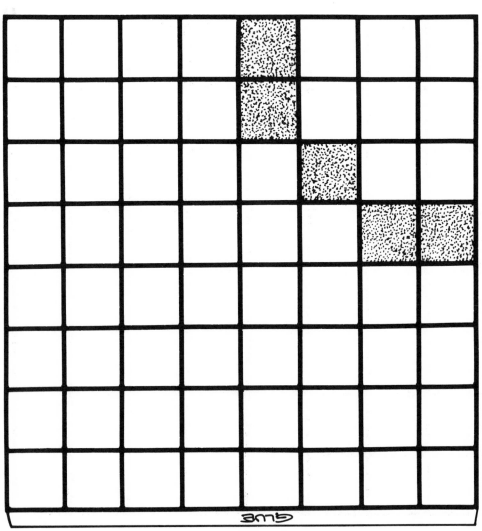

HALMA PLAYING-BOARD PATTERN.—3.

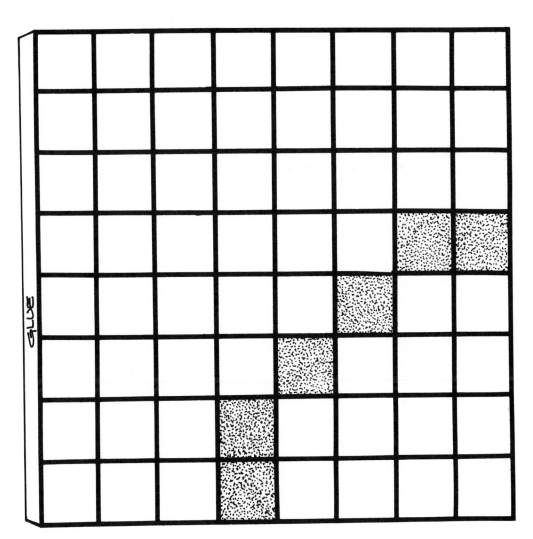

HALMA PLAYING-BOARD PATTERN.—4.

CHINESE CHECKERS

CHINESE CHECKERS is a simplified, faster version of Halma that became popular during the 1880s. Whether or not it was invented in China is not known, but it is played in the People's Republic of China today as well as in Europe and the United States.

March 18, 1941.   J. E. HUFFAKER   2,235,615
GAME BOARD
Filed March 28, 1940   2 Sheets—Sheet 1

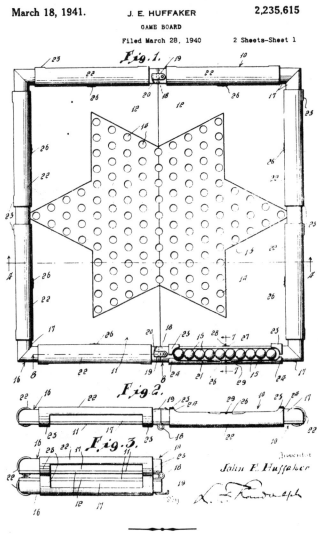

Fig. 1.

Fig. 2.

Fig. 3.

Inventor
John E. Huffaker

HOW TO PLAY CHINESE CHECKERS.

NUMBER OF PLAYERS.—Two, three, four, or six. When four or six people play, they may form partnerships.

OBJECTIVE.—To be the first player to move all of one's pieces into the opposite corner of the star board. When partners play, they both must move all of their pieces to the other's starting corner of the board.

MATERIALS.—A star-shaped playing board of six points, and sets of ten or 15 playing pieces, each set a different color.

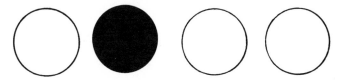

TO BEGIN PLAY.—Determine which player is to go first. If only two people are playing, they each place 15 pieces in opposite home bases, as shown below.

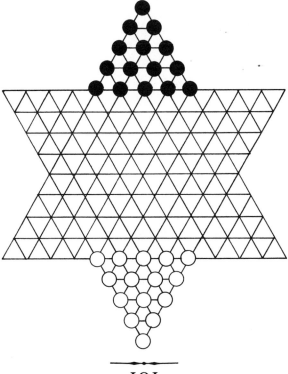

If three or more people play, set up the board with ten pieces for each player at alternate points of the star. If four or six play, each player places his or her pieces opposite an opponent or partner.

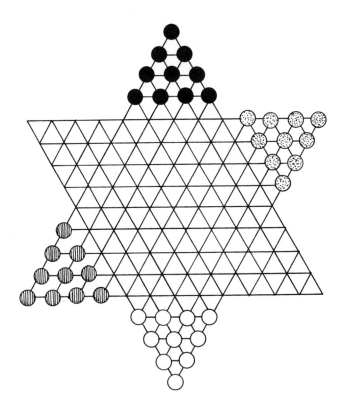

To Play.—Pieces are moved in much the same way as in Halma— either one step at a time in any direction along the connecting lines, or by jumping over one's own pieces and/or those of an opponent, as long as there is a vacant point to land on after each jump. As in Halma, a step move and a jump move may not be combined within the same turn. Pieces that are jumped are not removed from the board.

You may try to block or slow down your opponent's moves as in Halma, but be careful not to leave a piece off by itself where it can only make a single step move and slow down your own chances of winning the game.

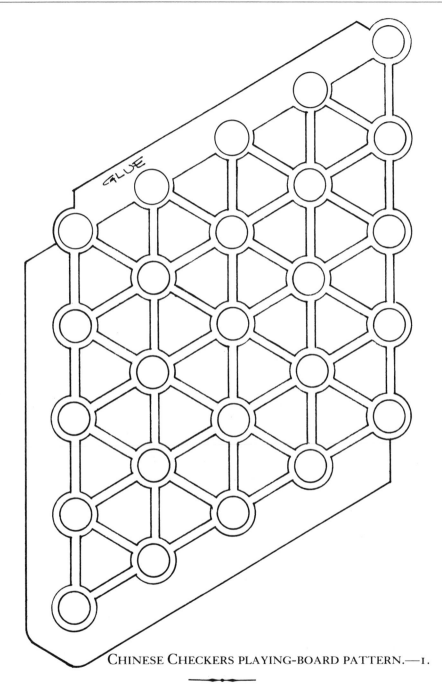

GLUE

CHINESE CHECKERS PLAYING-BOARD PATTERN.—1.

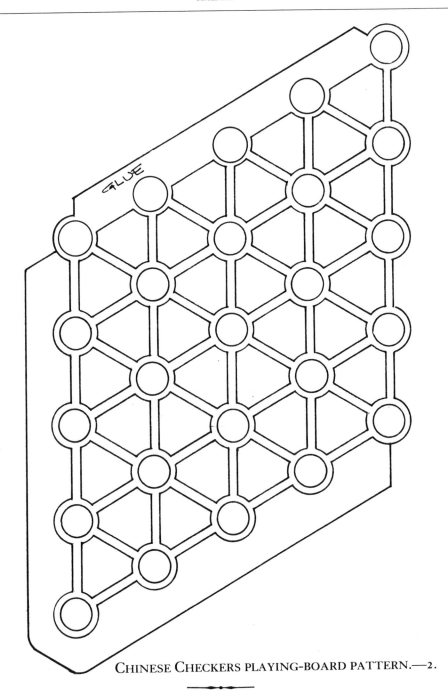

CHINESE CHECKERS PLAYING-BOARD PATTERN.—2.

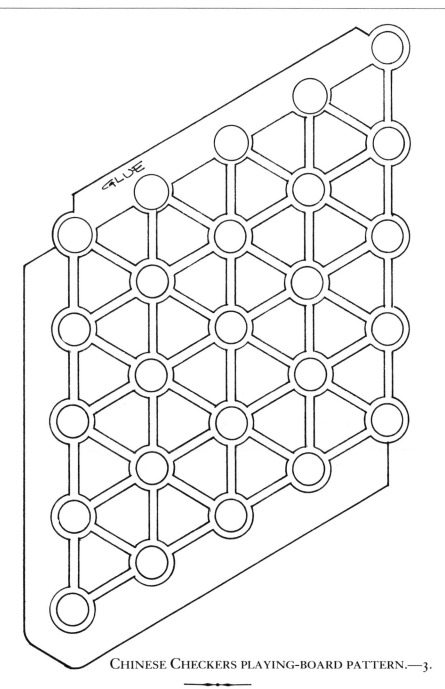

GLUE

CHINESE CHECKERS PLAYING-BOARD PATTERN.—3.

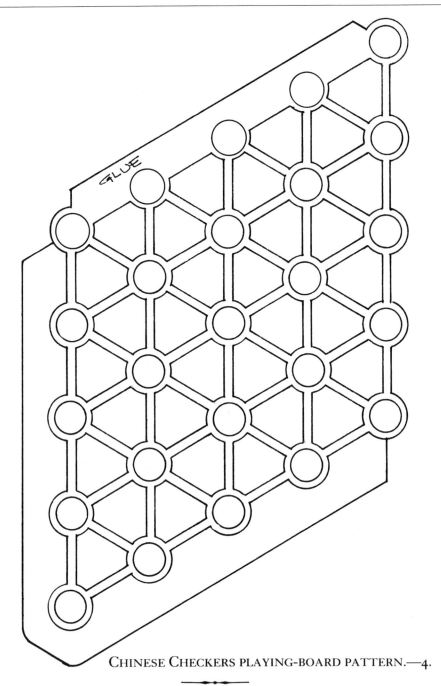

CHINESE CHECKERS PLAYING-BOARD PATTERN.—4.

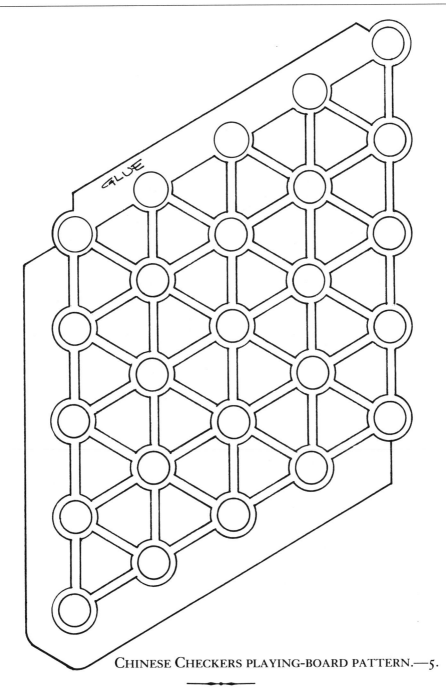

CHINESE CHECKERS PLAYING-BOARD PATTERN.—5.

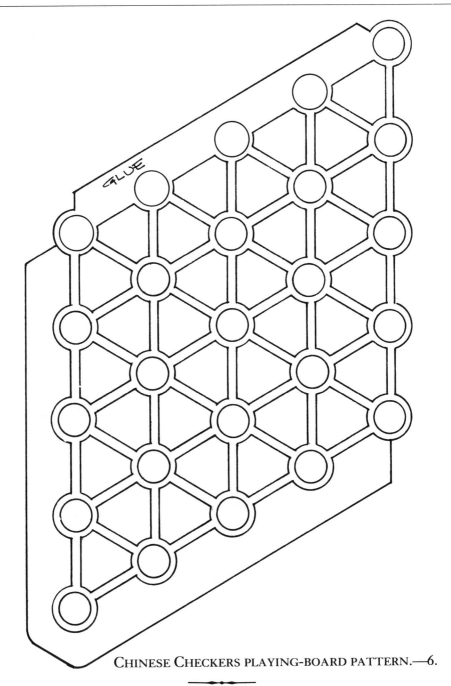

CHINESE CHECKERS PLAYING-BOARD PATTERN.—6.

MANCALA

WARI

Mancala games are some of the most intriguing and oldest two-player strategy games in the world. One version of these games, Kalaha, was played more than 7,000 years ago throughout Asia and Africa. Ancient boards for Kalaha can be found carved on the base of the columns of the Amon Temple at Karnak in Egypt and in the rock ledges along the ancient caravan routes. This provides clues as to how the game probably spread throughout the world.

Although the name and rules may vary from country to country, the boards and the strategy of the various Mancala games are closely related. All have simple rules to learn, but the strategies involved in winning the games are quite challenging!

Traditionally, Mancala games are played on a board carved out of wood with two rows of six playing cups each and two scoring cups. But the game is still played in some rural areas of the world by children and adults with simple pits scooped out of the ground. Perhaps the simplicity of Mancala boards partially explains why these games are so universally popular.

A MANCALA BOARD FROM THE MALDIVE
ISLANDS IN THE INDIAN OCEAN.

HOW TO PLAY MANCALA.

NUMBER OF PLAYERS.—Two.

OBJECTIVE.—Each player attempts to capture as many of the "seeds" or playing pieces as possible.

MATERIALS.—A playing board of two rows of six pits, two larger bins (*Kalahas*) at each end of the board, and 36 playing pieces or seeds.

To Begin Play.—Place three pieces or seeds in each pit and decide which player will take the first turn.

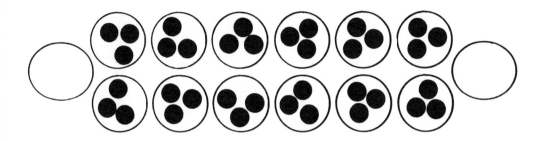

To Play.—The first player picks up all the pieces from any one of her six pits and sows the pieces, one in each pit, around the board counterclockwise, including in her own *Kalaha*. If there are enough pieces, the player continues sowing into the pits on the opponent's side of the board.

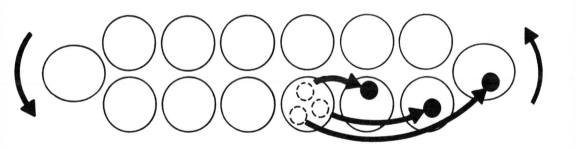

If a player's last piece lands in his own *Kalaha*, he gets another turn.

A player may capture the pieces in her opponent's pit if her last piece is sown in an empty pit on her own side of the board. The player then gets to capture all of the pieces in the opposite pit (her opponent's) and store them in her own *Kalaha* along with the capturing piece (her own).

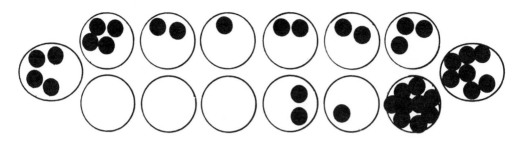

The dotted circles (below) indicate where nine playing pieces were before being moved into new pits.

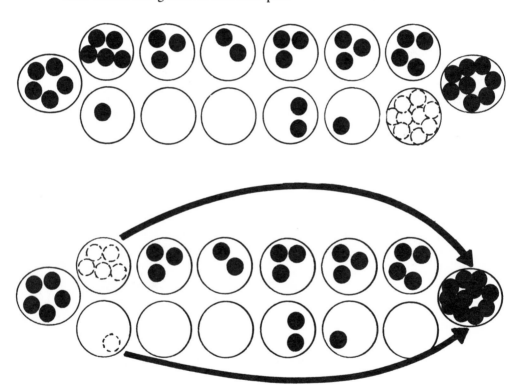

When all six pits on one side of the board are empty, the game is over. The player who still has playing pieces in his own pits gets to put them in his own *Kalaha*. The winner is the player with the most "seeds" or pieces in his or her own *Kalaha*.

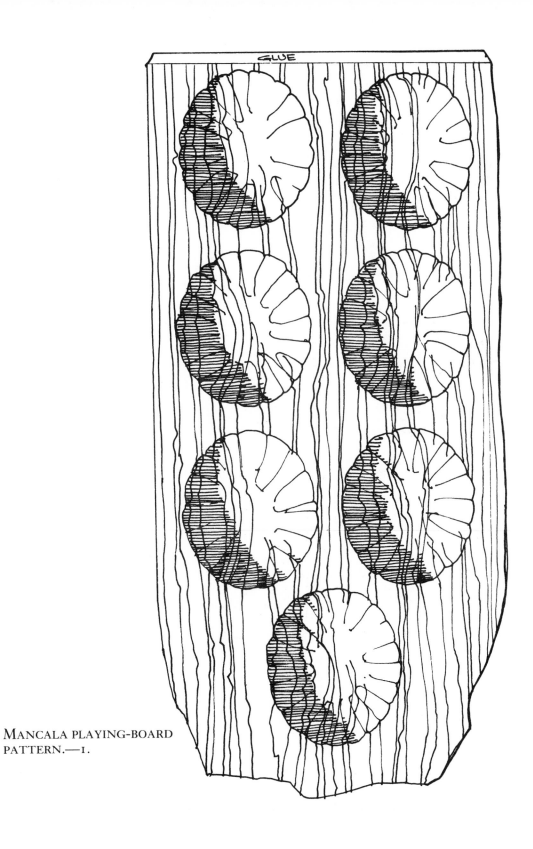

MANCALA PLAYING-BOARD
PATTERN.—I.

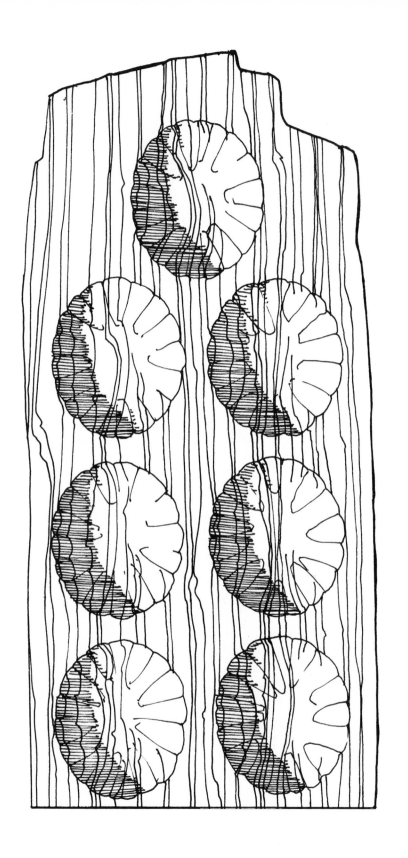

MANCALA
PLAYING-BOARD
PATTERN.—2.

WARI

WARI, another Mancala Game, is especially popular in Egypt and West Africa. Since each player has six more playing pieces than in Mancala and the rules are a bit more complicated, the possibilities for out-maneuvering your opponent are even more exciting.

April 3, 1951   M. B. LORENZANA ET AL   Des. 162,742

GAME BOARD

Filed Nov. 9, 1949

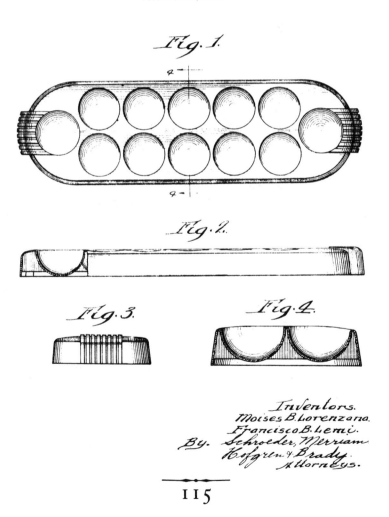

Fig. 1.

Fig. 2.

Fig. 3.   Fig. 4.

Inventors.
Moises B. Lorenzana.
Francisco B. Lemi.
By. Schroeder, Merriam
Hofgren & Brady.
Attorneys.

HOW TO PLAY WARI.

NUMBER OF PLAYERS.—Two.

OBJECTIVE.—Each player tries to capture as many "seeds" or playing pieces as possible.

MATERIALS.—A Mancala playing board (identical to the Mancala board) and 48 playing pieces or seeds.

TO BEGIN PLAY.—Place four pieces in each pit and decide which player will take the first turn.

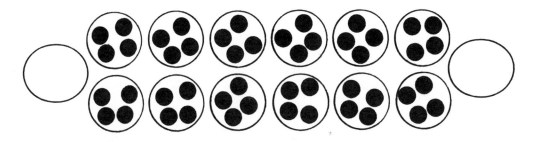

TO PLAY.—The first player picks up all of the pieces in one of her pits and sows them, one in each pit, around the board counterclockwise. Unlike in Mancala, no pieces are placed in the large pits, or *Kalahas*, at each end of the board. These bins are used only to store captured pieces.

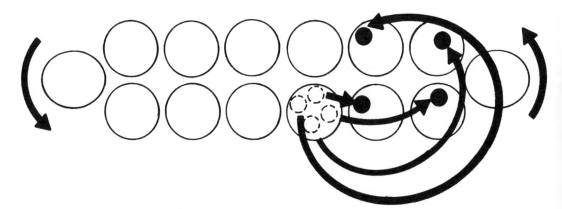

If there are more than 12 pieces in a player's pit, then she will have to sow the pieces from that pit completely around the board. In this case, the emptied pit is passed over when completing the sowing.

When an opponent's pits are empty, a player must, if possible, make a move that provides the opponent with a piece to play with. If the player fails to do so, he forfeits all of his pieces to the opponent. If it is impossible to provide the opponent with a piece, then the game ends and all of the pieces left on the board go into the player's *Kalaha*.

A player may capture pieces in her opponent's pits by placing the last piece of a move into an opponent's pit that already holds one or two pieces. If the pits that precede this pit also contain two or three pieces in an unbroken sequence, then the pieces in these pits are also captured.

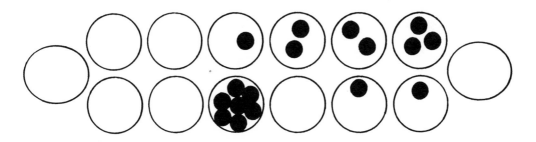

The dotted circles (below) indicate where seven pieces were before being moved into new pits.

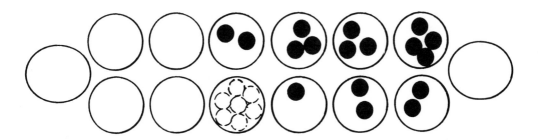

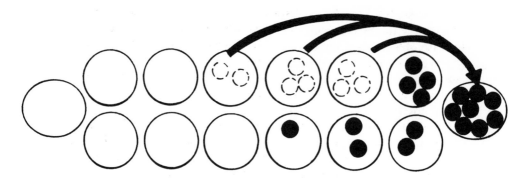

A player cannot capture all of the opponent's pieces, since this would make it impossible for each player to alternate turns.

The game ends when it is no longer possible for either player to capture any of the opponent's pieces. Each player adds the pieces left in the pits on his or her side of the board to his or her own store (*Kalaha*), and the player with the largest number of pieces is the winner.

STEEPLECHASE

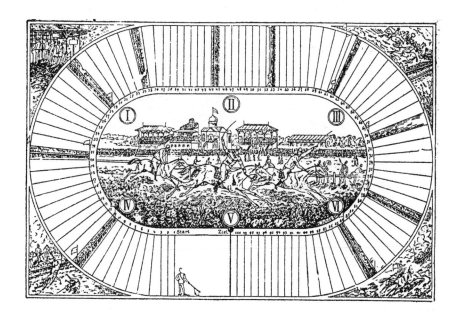

STEEPLECHASE was one of the most popular nineteenth-century versions of the Royal Game of Goose. The game first appeared in England about 1850, where it was played on an oval race course with cardboard horses and riders mounted on stands. But instead of death's heads and bridges representing bad luck, obstacles such as jumps, hurdles, ditches, fences, and hedges appeared along the race course. The horses and riders were moved around the track according to the spin of a teetotum or the roll of a six-sided die. The player who moved his horse around the track to the finish line first, dodging and overcoming all obstacles, was the winner. Bets were often placed on the outcome of the race, just like in real horse racing.

The popularity of Steeplechase undoubtedly encouraged the development of other types of racing games during the second half of the nineteenth century. Since many of the early race games were printed by map makers, their journeys often wove their way over boards that were actually maps. The board for "An Eccentric Excursion to the Chinese Empire," one of the most popular early race games published by the William Spooner Company in England in the 1840s, was decorated with all sorts of exciting mishaps and adventures, including a flight in Henson's steam-powered airplane! More-modern versions of the game included automobiles, boats, and even airplanes racing one another.

HOW TO PLAY
STEEPLECHASE.

NUMBER OF PLAYERS.—Two to six.

OBJECTIVE.—To be the first player to complete the race by passing the last square on the board, which is the finish line.

MATERIALS.—A round or oval playing-board race course divided into playing spaces, some of which are designated as obstacles. A six-sided teetotum or die and a playing piece of a different color for each player are also needed.

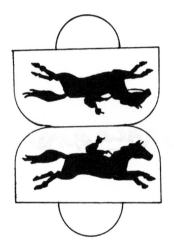 

PATTERN FOR STEEPLECHASE
PLAYING PIECE.

TO BEGIN PLAY.—Each player spins the teetotum or throws the die to see who gets the highest number and goes first. The other players take their turns according to the number they threw, with the highest going second and so on.

TO PLAY.—Each player's piece is moved according to the number shown on the teetotum or die. If a player lands on a square marked with a fence or hurdle, which appear at intervals along the race course (squares 3, 9, 15, 28, 33, 40, and 54), then she loses her next turn. The first player to pass the final square or finish line wins the race.

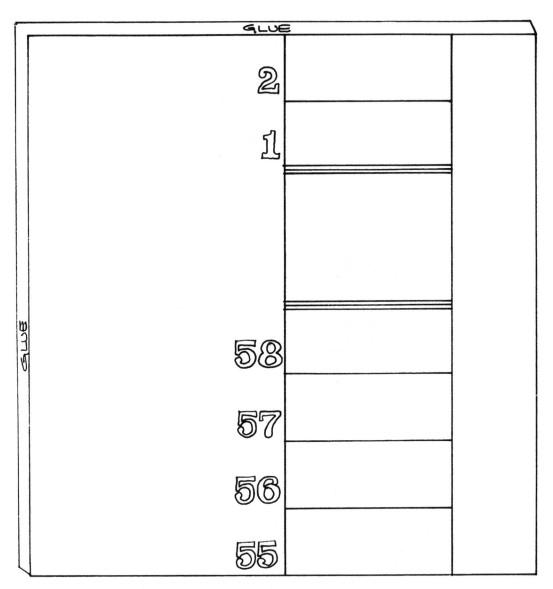

STEEPLECHASE PLAYING-BOARD PATTERN.—1.

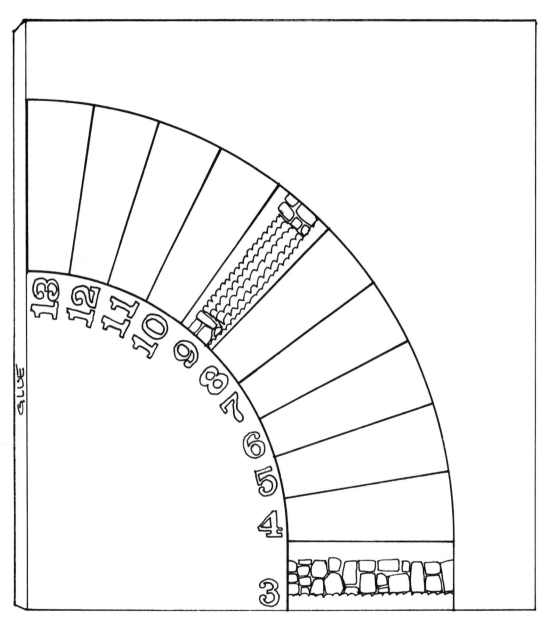

STEEPLECHASE PLAYING-BOARD PATTERN.—2.

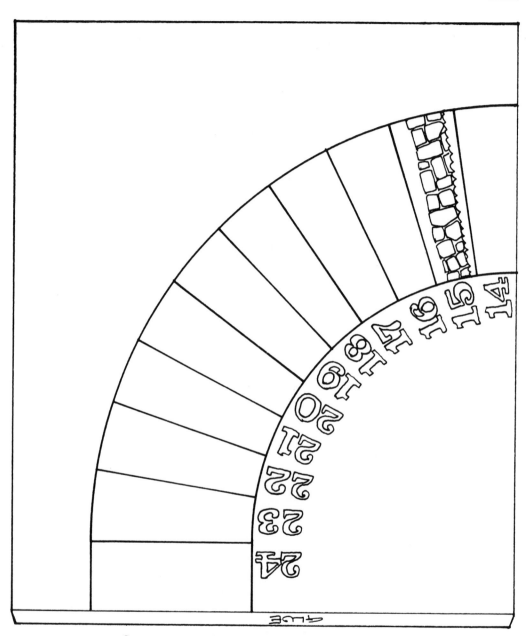

STEEPLECHASE PLAYING-BOARD PATTERN.—3.

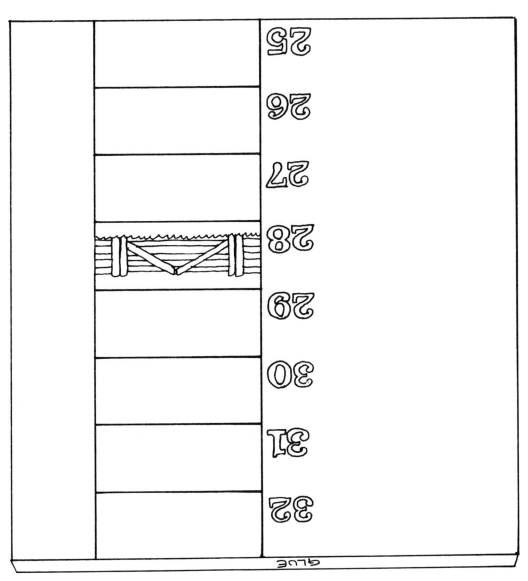

STEEPLECHASE PLAYING-BOARD PATTERN.—4.

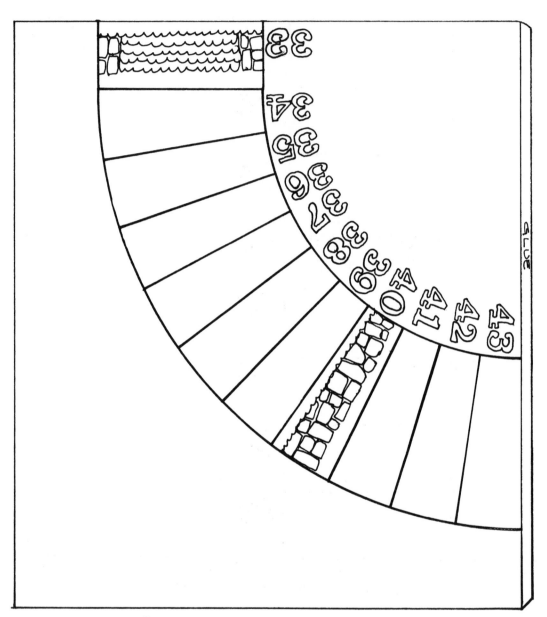

STEEPLECHASE PLAYING-BOARD PATTERN.—5.

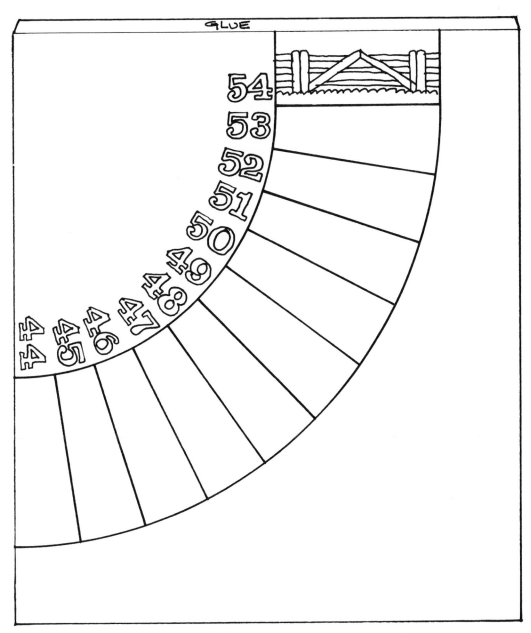

STEEPLECHASE PLAYING-BOARD PATTERN.—6.

QUEEN'S GUARD

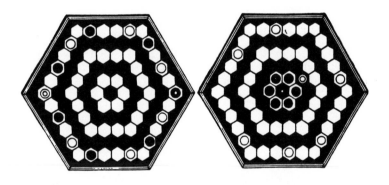

QUEEN'S GUARD, also known as *Agon*, was a popular board game during the Victorian Era that combined the complexity of the strategy in Chess with the simplicity of the moves in Checkers. The game is won when one of the players positions his Queen in the center of the board surrounded by her attending guard of six pieces.

HOW TO PLAY
QUEEN'S GUARD.

NUMBER OF PLAYERS.—Two.

OBJECTIVE.—To be the first player to place your Queen in the board's central space and surround her by your other six pieces (the Queen's guards).

MATERIALS.—A hexagonal playing board made up of 91 smaller hexagons. Each player has seven playing pieces whose color is distinct from those of their opponent's pieces. One of these pieces is specially designated as a Queen. The remaining six pieces are guards.

TO BEGIN PLAY.—After determining which player is to go first, you can begin the game in two different ways. In the first, the Queens (represented in the following illustration by square pieces) are placed in opposite corners, with each player's guards taking alternating positions around the outer rim of the board, as shown at the top of page 131.

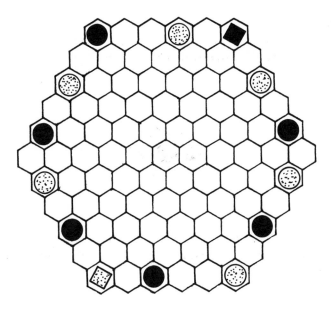

In the second version, each player takes alternate turns placing his or her pieces wherever they like on the outer rim of the board.

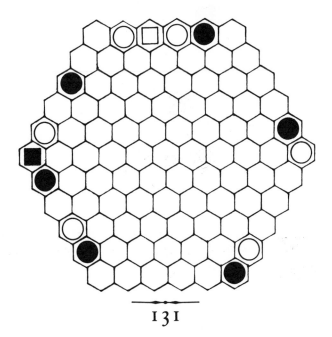

Pieces are moved one space forward or sideways. Once a piece has been moved toward the center, it may not be moved backwards toward the outer rim. If a player touches a piece, he must move it or forfeit his turn.

To Play.—When a guard is trapped between an opponent's pieces, its player must move it to any vacant space on the outer rim of the board in her next turn.

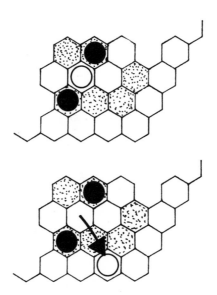

When a player's Queen is trapped between two of the opponent's pieces, the player must move his Queen to any vacant hexagon chosen by the opponent for his next turn.

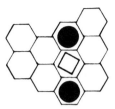

If more than one piece is trapped in a single turn, the player must continue to use her turns until all of the trapped pieces have been returned to the outermost ring of the board. Guards may be returned to the outer ring in any order, but if a Queen and a guard are captured together, the Queen must be moved first.

Only a Queen can be placed in the central hexagon. The game is forefeited by a player if the central hexagon is empty and he encloses it with six of his guards, as shown below.

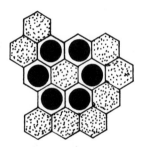

The game is won when a player places her Queen in the central hexagon on the board and surrounds her with her six guards.

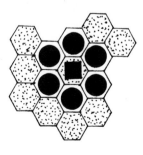

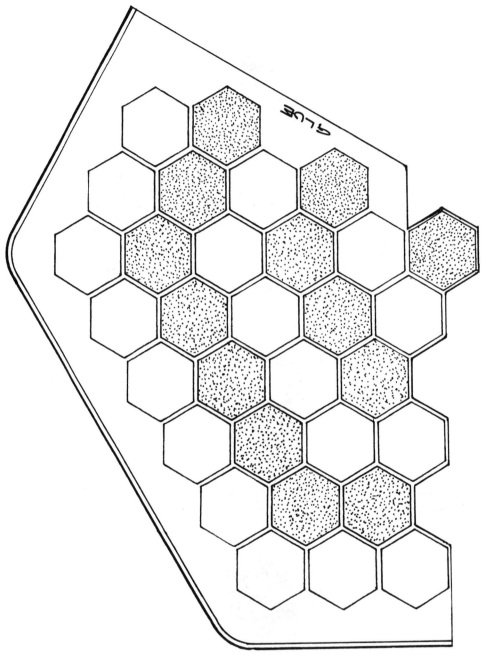

QUEEN'S GUARD PLAYING-BOARD PATTERN.—I.

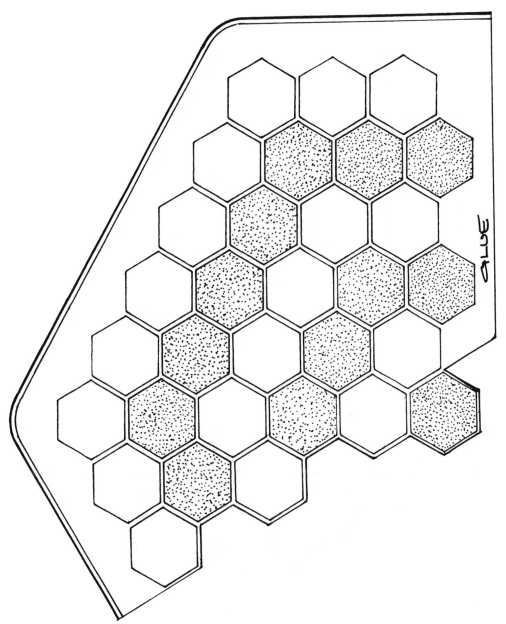

QUEEN'S GUARD PLAYING-BOARD PATTERN.—2.

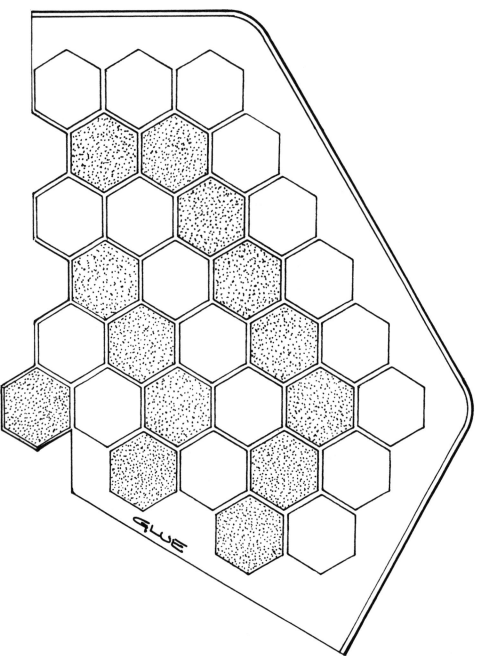

GLUE

QUEEN'S GUARD PLAYING-BOARD PATTERN.—3.

CHIVALRY

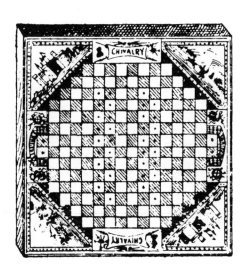

CHIVALRY was one of the many battle games manufactured by Parker Brothers of Salem, Massachusetts, during the late 1880s. Included among these games were such titles as the "Battle of Manila," "Waterloo," "Trafalgar," and "Roosevelt's Charge." But it was Chivalry that the Parker Brothers Catalogue described as the best board game invented in 2,000 years!

THE 1930 PATENT FOR CAMELOT, A SIMPLIFIED VERSION OF CHIVALRY.

Oct. 28, 1930.   G. S. PARKER   1,780,038

GAME

Filed Jan. 28, 1930   3 Sheets—Sheet 2

Fig.2.

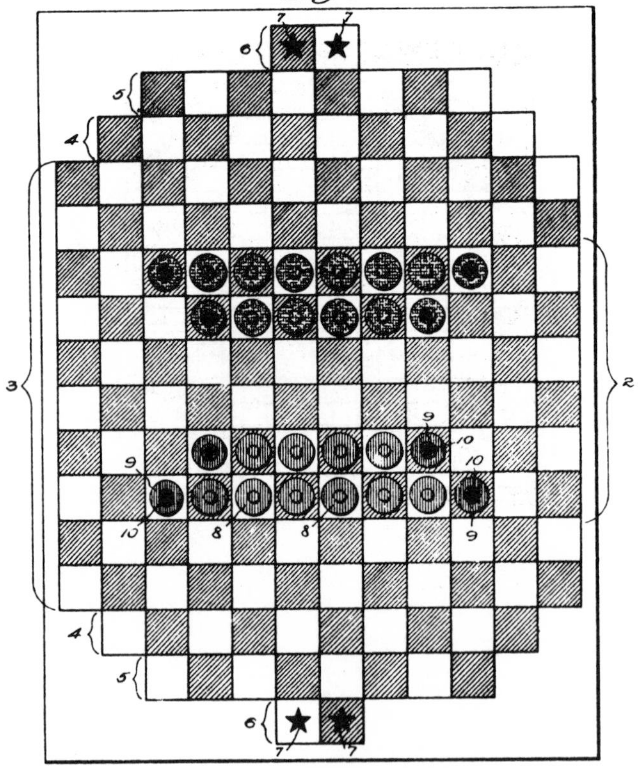

Inventor:
George S. Parker
by Emery, Booth, Varney & Townsend Attys

138

In Chivalry, each one of the players has an army of eight knights and 12 pawns with which they try to capture the opponent's pieces and occupy his stronghold to win the game. Although the knights and pawns can make different moves, as in Chess, Chivalry is a much simpler game to learn. Despite its simplicity, the number of tactical possibilities in the one-to-one battle between players in Chivalry makes it as exciting and stimulating as the most complicated board games.

Parker Brothers introduced a simplified version of Chivalry known as Camelot in 1930. But neither Chivalry nor this new version of the game was able to attain the original game's popularity, for both were superseded by a revived interest in the even older game of Backgammon.

HOW TO PLAY CHIVALRY.

NUMBER OF PLAYERS.—Two.

OBJECTIVE.—To be the first player to occupy the stronghold spaces on your opponent's side of the board with any two of your own pieces.

MATERIALS.—An irregularly shaped playing board of 176 squares. Both player's stronghold spaces are marked with stars or xs on opposite sides of the playing board. Each player has 12 playing pieces that are pawns and eight pieces designated as knights. All the pieces are of a different color from their opponent's pieces.

TO BEGIN PLAY.—Place each player's pieces on the board as illustrated at the top of page 140 and decide which player will take the first turn.

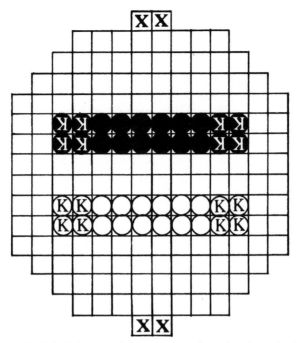

To Play.—Both knights and pawns can move in three basic ways:

● By moving one space in any direction, but not diagonally.

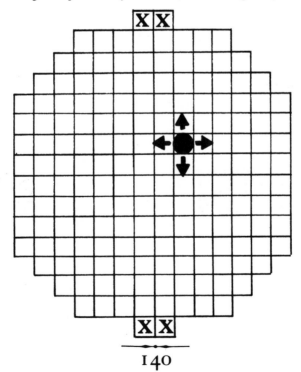

○ By "cantoring," or leaping over, one of your own pieces to a vacant space on the other side. Players may leap over as many of their own pieces as possible within one turn. A player does not have to make a cantor move if one is possible.

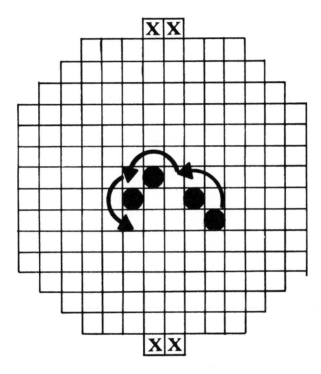

● Or, by jumping over an opponent's piece in any direction to a vacant space on the other side (see next page). When an opponent's piece is jumped, it is removed from the board. A player must make a jump move whenever possible and must continue jumping all the pieces possible within one turn.

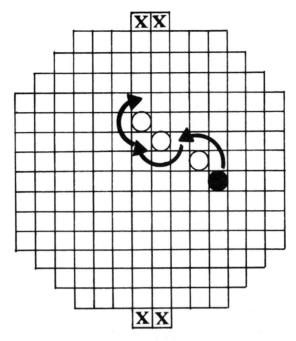

Pawns can make any of the three moves described but cannot combine any of them within one turn. Knights can combine cantoring over one of their own pieces with jumping an opponent's piece or pieces, but all of the cantor moves must be made before the jumps.

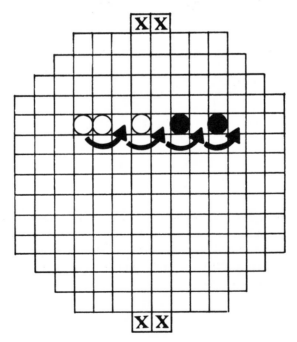

A knight cannot combine the basic move of advancing one space in any direction with a cantor or jump move.

The first player to succeed in placing any two of her pieces in her opponent's two stronghold spaces on the opposite side of the board wins the game.

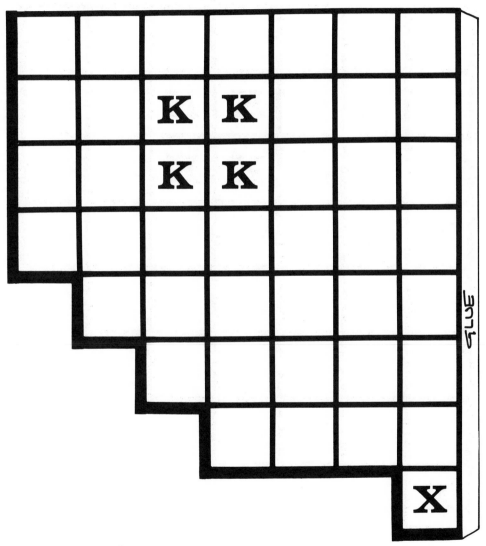

CHIVALRY PLAYING-BOARD PATTERN.—I.

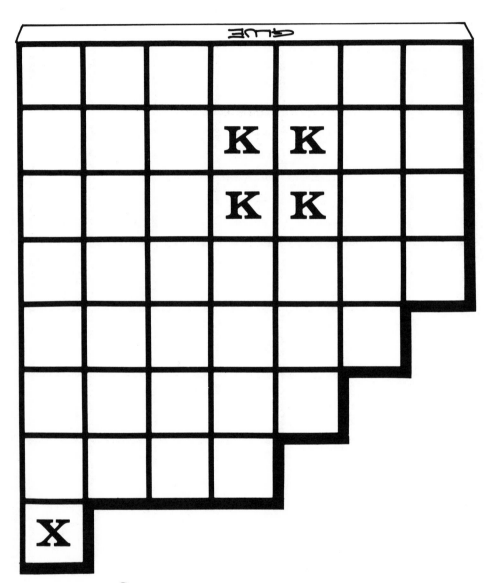

CHIVALRY PLAYING-BOARD PATTERN.—2.

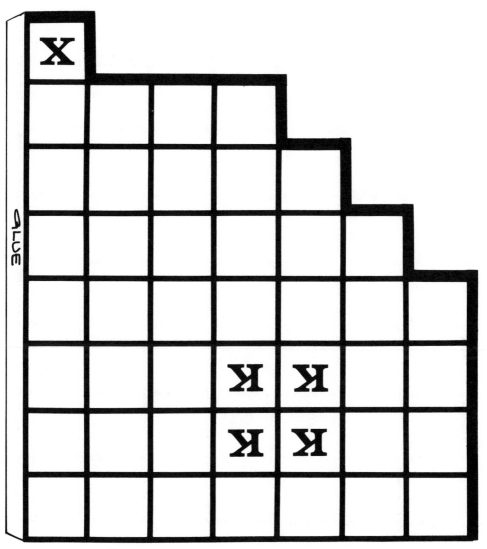

CHIVALRY PLAYING-BOARD PATTERN.—3.

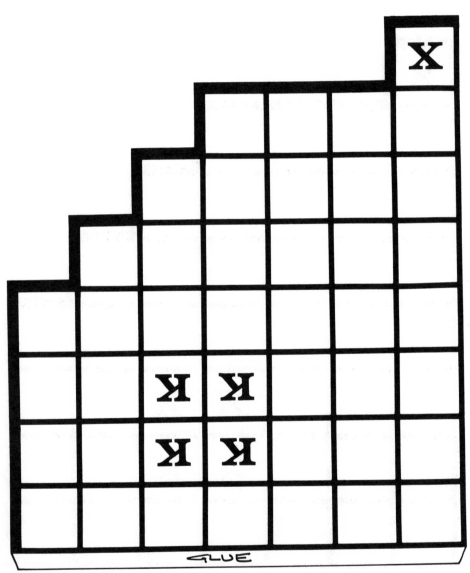

CHIVALRY PLAYING-BOARD PATTERN.—4.

GO-BANG

HASAMI SHOGI
DARA

W. B. SILVER.

GAME BOARD.

No. 255,892.   Patented Apr. 4, 1882.

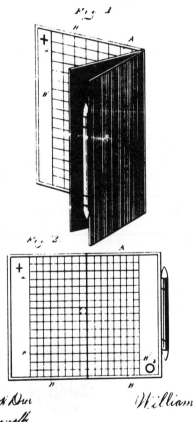

WITNESSES

Charles N. Dun

W. E. Donnelly

INVENTOR

William B. Silver

GO-BANG, a great strategy game for two players, originated in Japan, where it is called *Go-Moku*. The game is played on the same board as *Go*, which is believed to be one of the oldest games in the world, having been invented in China more than three thousand years ago. Since both players are constantly attacking and defending their positions all over the board, the game can be very exciting and complicated. As seen in the patent by W. B. Silver (page 147), Go-Bang was not only a popular board game in America during the nineteenth century, but it was also commonly played on slates such as the one invented by Mr. Silver, which could be folded and carried in a pocket.

HOW TO PLAY GO-BANG.

NUMBER OF PLAYERS.—Two.

OBJECTIVE.—To form a straight line of five playing pieces, either vertically, horizontally, or diagonally.

MATERIALS.—The traditional Japanese Go table ("Go-ban"), a large square marked off in a grid of 18 squares on each side, is made of wood and is stained yellow. There are 361 points of intersecting lines on which the game is played.

Go-Bang can also be played on a simpler board of 100 squares, ten on each side. When playing on a board of 100 squares, each player places his or her pieces on the squares instead of on the points of intersecting lines. This is the version that will be explained on the following pages.

Each player has a set of 50 playing pieces, with each player's set being of a different color from his opponent's.

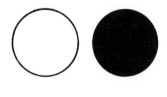

To Begin Play.—The players decide who will play with which color of pieces. The dark pieces always take the first turn. The playing pieces are placed anywhere on the board, one each turn in alternating turns.

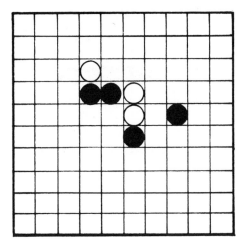

To Play.—Once a piece has been placed on a square on the board, it cannot be moved until the end of the game. In order to win, players must place five pieces in a row, vertically, horizontally, or diagonally.

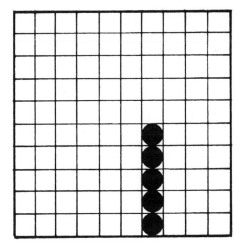

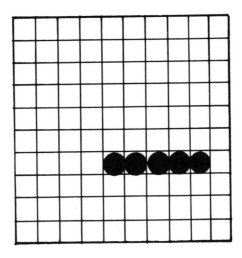

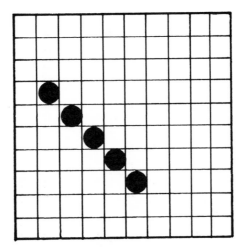

If neither player has succeeded in forming a "five" before all the pieces are placed on the board, then the game ends in a draw.

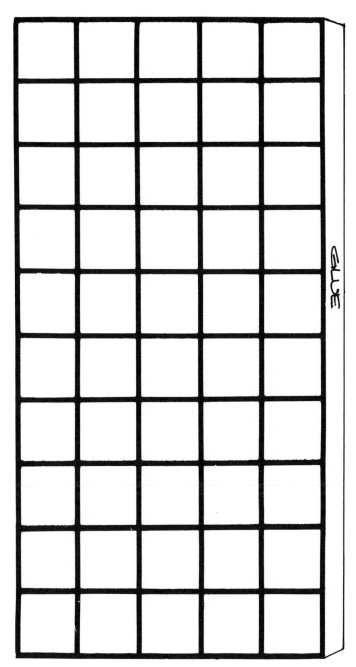

GO-BANG PLAYING-BOARD PATTERN.—I.

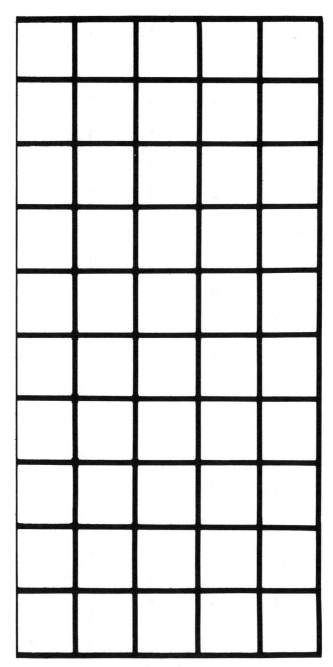

GO-BANG PLAYING-BOARD PATTERN.—2.

HASAMI SHOGI

HASAMI SHOGI, another variation of Go-Bang, is a very popular children's game in Japan. Played on a board similar to a Go board, the game quickly becomes exciting as both players not only try to capture their opponent's pieces, but also try to prevent their opponent from forming a row of nine pieces. At the same time, they are trying to form their own row of nine pieces. This makes the game a fast-paced combination of blocking, attacking, and out-witting your opponent.

HOW TO PLAY
HASAMI SHOGI.

NUMBER OF PLAYERS.—Two.

OBJECTIVE.—To be the first player to complete a row of nine pieces in any direction anywhere on the board, except the two rows designated as your own home base. At the same time, each player tries to capture as many of the opponent's pieces as possible to prevent the opponent from completing a row of nine pieces.

MATERIALS.—A square playing board divided into 81 squares, nine on each side. Each player has 18 playing pieces with one player's set being a different color from the opponents'.

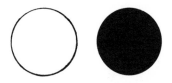

TO BEGIN PLAY.—Each player places his or her 18 pieces on the board, as illustrated at the top of page 154, and decides which player will take the first turn.

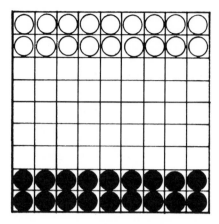

To Play.—Each player may move one piece per turn in any direction, except diagonally.

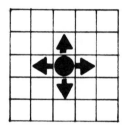

A piece may be moved to a vacant adjacent square or may jump over a piece, either the player's or the opponent's, to a vacant square next to it.

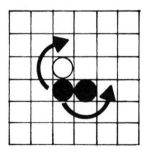

Jumped pieces are not removed from the board. No more than one jump is permitted per turn.

An opponent's piece may be captured and removed from the board if a player's piece can be moved so that it traps the opponent's piece between two of the player's pieces, or traps the opponent's piece in one of the corners of the board. A piece is not captured if it is diagonally flanked by two of the opponent's pieces.

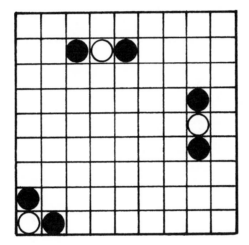

A player's piece is not considered captured if the player moves it onto a vacant square between two of the opponent's pieces.

The game is won by a player's either capturing all of his or her opponent's pieces, or by successfully moving nine pieces into a row, horizontally or vertically, anywhere on the board except along the player's own two home base rows. If a player captures at least ten of the opponent's pieces, it is impossible for the opponent to form a row of nine pieces. But even if ten or more of your pieces are captured, you may still prevent your opponent from forming a row of nine pieces or you may even capture all of your opponent's pieces and win the game!

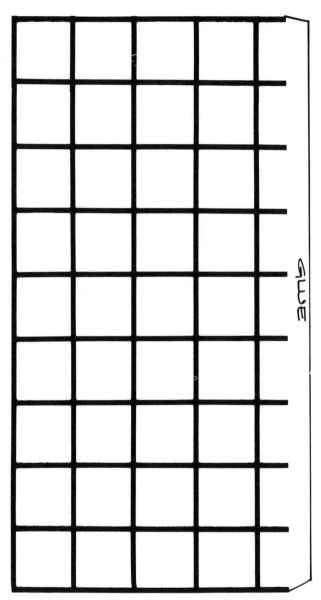

Hᴀsᴀᴍɪ Sʜᴏɢɪ ᴘʟᴀʏɪɴɢ-ʙᴏᴀʀᴅ ᴘᴀᴛᴛᴇʀɴ.—ɪ.

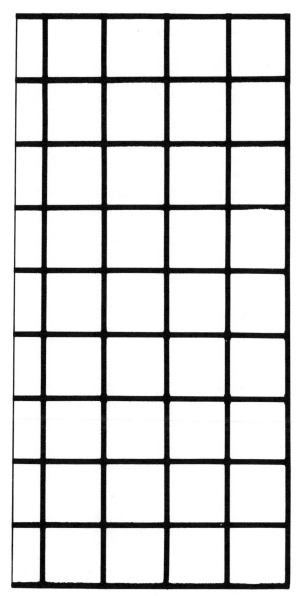

HASAMI SHOGI PLAYING-BOARD PATTERN.—2.

DARA

DARA (or Derrah), a popular North African version of Go-Bang, is usually played on a wooden board with thirty pits. Pebbles, beans, or marbles are used as playing pieces. Since the game is played in two phases, it involves both strategic planning and the concentration necessary to both block and out-maneuver your opponent.

In the first phase, the players place their twelve playing pieces on the board wherever they choose; however, no more than two pieces of the same color may be next to each other. In the second phase, players take turns moving their pieces, trying to get three in a row. This gives them the right to remove one of their opponent's pieces from the board.

Dara can be played on a board with pits, on a board marked with 30 squares, or even on the ground in hollows dug out of the earth.

HOW TO PLAY DARA.

NUMBER OF PLAYERS.—Two.

OBJECTIVE.—Each player tries to move his or her pieces so that they form a row of three, which entitles them to remove one of the opponent's pieces. When one player is no longer able to form a row of three pieces or when all of one player's pieces have been removed from the board, the game ends and the other player is the winner.

MATERIALS.—A rectangular playing board divided into 30 squares, six on one side and five on the other. Each player has 12 playing pieces; one player has one color and the other player has another color.

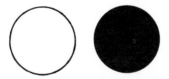

TO BEGIN PLAY.—After deciding which player will take the first turn, the players alternate placing their pieces on any square of the board. No more than two pieces may be placed next to each other by the same player during the first phase of the game.

Since the placement of pieces during this part of the game will determine which moves will be possible during the second phase, it is important to plan carefully where to place the pieces.

To PLAY.—After all of the 24 pieces are on the board, each player may move one piece one square per turn, backward, forward, or sideways, but not diagonally.

Neither player may set more than three pieces in a row. Rows of four pieces do not count or allow a player to remove the opponent's piece from the board.

DARA PLAYING-BOARD PATTERN.

SEEGA

SEEGA is the modern version of Senat, one of the most ancient games of skill. As in many other very old board games, pieces are captured by being confined on two sides. But in Seega, the pieces are not arranged on the board at the beginning of play. Instead, they are placed on the board alternatively by each player, so great foresight and planning are required to be sure that your pieces occupy the most strategic positions to complete the game and win.

Although the rules for Senat have not survived, we know that it was played in Egypt nearly 5,000 years ago. In fact, four different Senat boards were found in the tomb of the Pharoah Tutankhamon (c. 1347–1339 B.C.) when it was discovered in 1922. Seega is played on a smaller board than Senat, and with fewer pieces.

Today, the modern game of Seega is popular in Egypt and North Africa, where it is often played on a board drawn on and scooped out of the sand. Pebbles, beans, or small pieces of wood are used as playing pieces. They are called *kelbs*, or "dogs."

HOW TO PLAY SEEGA.

NUMBER OF PLAYERS.—Two.

OBJECTIVE.—To capture all of the opponent's pieces or to block them so that they cannot move.

MATERIALS.—A square playing board divided into 25 squares, and 12 playing pieces. Each player uses a different color. The game may also be played on a board of 49 or 81 squares. In each case, the number of playing pieces is increased to total one less than the total number of squares on the board.

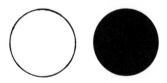

TO BEGIN PLAY.—The players decide who will take the first turn. The first player places two pieces on any squares of the board, except on the center square. The second player then does the same, and they continue placing two pieces per turn until all of the pieces are on the board. The center square is always left vacant.

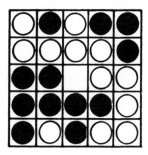

To Play.—The last player to place two pieces on the board makes the first move, moving one piece forward or backward, but never diagonally. Obviously, the first move must be made into the center square. But if the first player to move a piece is unable to do so because the opponent's pieces are blocking the center square, then one of the opponent's pieces is removed.

A player may capture an opponent's piece by flanking or confining it on both sides with two of their own pieces, horizontally or vertically, but not diagonally.

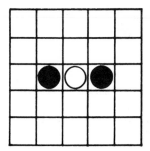 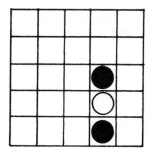

Captures can only be made after all of the playing pieces have been placed on the board. A player may capture more than one of the opponent's pieces if by continuing to move *the same piece*, the player can again flank one of the opponent's pieces, as shown on page 164.

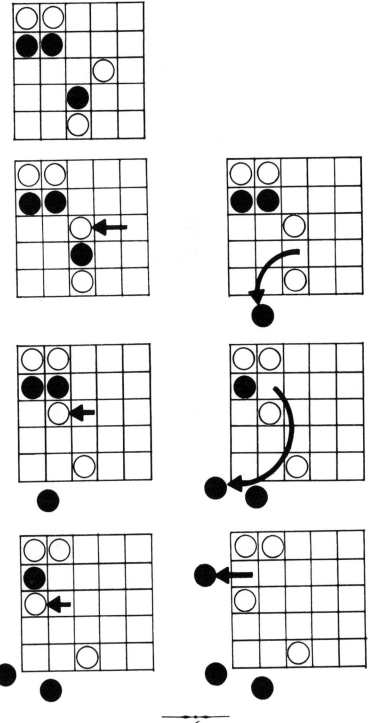

Likewise, a player may capture more than one of the opponent's pieces by moving into the position shown below.

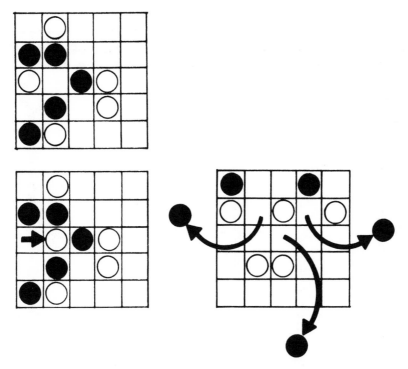

A player can move his or her own piece into a square between two of the opponent's pieces without being captured.

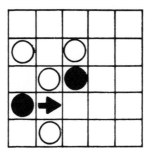

If a player becomes blocked and cannot move a piece, the opponent takes another turn.

The game is over when one player captures all the other player's pieces or when one player's pieces are completely blocked and unable to move. If both players are blocked, the game ends in a draw.

SEEGA PLAYING-BOARD PATTERN.

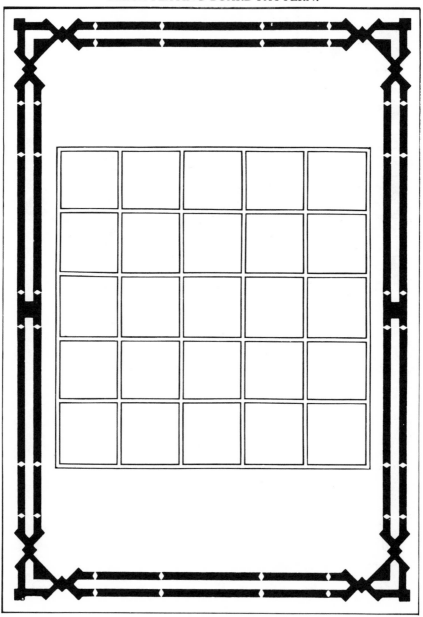

FOX AND GEESE

ASALTO
THE CHINESE REBEL GAME
HARE AND HOUNDS

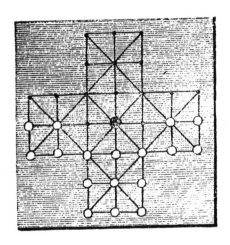

FOX AND GEESE, an intriguing contest between two unequal opponents, has been a favorite game throughout Europe since the Middle Ages. Even though the Geese outnumber the Fox in this hunt game, they are more restricted in the moves they can make and must try to capture the Fox by crowding it into a corner where it cannot move. But the Fox has a different objective. It tries to capture as many of the Geese as possible to prevent its own capture. If careful in their strategic chasing of the Fox, the Geese should always win the game.

Not only does a description of Fox and Geese appear in the *Grettis Saga*, an Icelandic poem written about A.D. 1300, but also in the household accounts of Edward IV of England (1461–83), who purchased two Fox and Geese sets made of silver. English royalty was still playing the game during the nineteenth century, and it is known to have been a favorite of Queen Victoria and Prince Albert.

The tactical possibilities in Fox and Geese make it a popular game not only in Europe but in the Orient and North America as well. Japanese call the game *juroku musashi*, or "sixteen soldiers." In their version, 16 soldiers try to surround their general. Among the Indians of the Southwestern United States, a coyote tries to outwit the chickens, or a jack rabbit attempts to escape Indian hunters. The Cree and Chippewa Indians of Canada also played Fox and Geese but called it *musinaykahwhan-metowaywin.*

Fox and Geese is one of the many board games included in this book that were often played outdoors with their board inscribed on stone or in clay, or drawn on the ground. It is also a popular game often played by children on playgrounds or in the snow, where a number of concentric circles, crisscrossed with straight lines, are drawn.

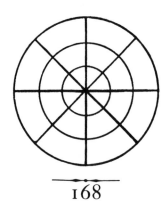

Just as in the board game, the Geese have greater flexibility. The player who is picked to be the Fox can only run along the straight lines, but the Geese can run along any of the paths. On the playground, the game is really tag, for if the Fox touches a Goose, that Goose must become the Fox.

HOW TO PLAY FOX AND GEESE.

NUMBER OF PLAYERS.—Two.

OBJECTIVE.—The Geese try to trap the Fox so that it cannot move, and the Fox tries to capture as many of the Geese as possible so that they cannot surround it.

MATERIALS.—A cross-shaped board with 33 holes or spaces connected by straight and diagonal lines. Seventeen playing pieces of one color for the Geese and one piece of another color for the Fox are used.

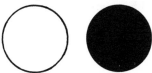

TO BEGIN PLAY.—Place the pieces on the board as illustrated below. The Fox is usually placed in the center, as shown, but it may be placed on any vacant spot the player chooses.

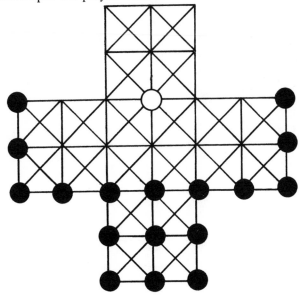

To Play.—The Fox always takes the first turn. It is able to move in any direction: forward, backward, diagonally, or sideways, along the connecting lines.

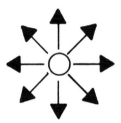

The Fox tries to capture the Geese by jumping over them into a free space on the board. It may capture more than one Goose in one move as long as there is an empty space for it to land on next to each Goose that is captured. The captured Geese are all removed from the board.

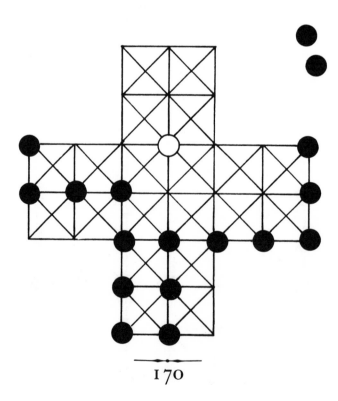

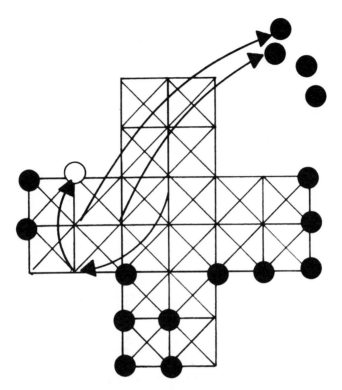

If it has no other move, the Fox must jump a Goose even if it lands on a vulnerable spot.

The Geese may move forward, to the side, or diagonally along the connecting lines, but never backward.

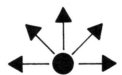

Geese may not jump over the Fox but must try to surround or trap it instead.

The Fox and Geese alternate turns. The Geese try to win by crowding the Fox into a corner so that it cannot move. The Fox can win by capturing so many of the Geese that they cannot surround it or by forcing all the Geese to move forward to the other side of the board so that they no longer have a move and can't chase it.

FOX AND GEESE PLAYING-BOARD PATTERN.—I.

FOX AND GEESE PLAYING-BOARD PATTERN.—2.

ASALTO

ASALTO ("Assault"), one of the variations of Fox and Geese, is also a contest between two unequal opponents who try to block, out-maneuver, and outwit each other. In this game, a large but poorly armed force attacks a small but powerful fortress. Asalto is played on a board that is the same as the Fox and Geese board, but nine points are separated from the others and designated as the fortress.

One player occupies the fortress with two playing pieces—the officers (or sharpshooters). The other player has 24 pieces, or the foot soldiers, which occupy the surrounding points on the board, which are the battlefield. In order to win the game, these soldiers try to trap the two officers in the fortress, pen them anywhere on the battlefield so that they cannot move, or occupy every point within the fortress. If the officers capture so many foot soldiers that these maneuvers are impossible, they win the game.

An exciting variation of Asalto is Siege, which is played on a larger board that makes the game even more challenging.

HOW TO PLAY ASALTO.

NUMBER OF PLAYERS.—Two.

OBJECTIVE.—The 24 foot soldiers try to trap the officers inside the fortress or on the battlefield or try to occupy every point in the fortress. The officers try to capture so many of the foot soldiers (at least 15) that they cannot possibly trap them in the fortress or on the battlefield.

MATERIALS.—A cross-shaped playing board with 33 holes or spaces that are connected by straight and diagonal lines. Nine of these holes, all in one arm of the cross, are separated and designated as the fortress. Twenty-four playing pieces of one color for the foot soldiers and two pieces of another color for the officers or sharpshooters are used for the game.

To Begin Play.—Arrange the pieces on the board as illustrated below. The sharpshooters or officers may stand anywhere within the fort at the beginning of the game.

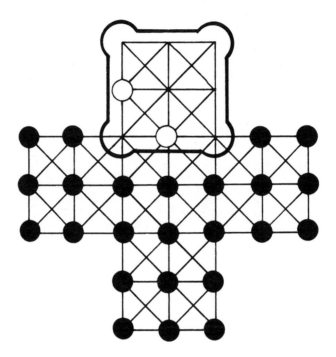

After you decide which player will play the foot soldiers and which will be the sharpshooters, the sharpshooters move first.

To Play.—As in Fox and Geese, the officers may move in any direction along the connecting lines, one space at a time. An officer or sharpshooter may capture a foot soldier by jumping over it to the next space, if it is vacant. The sharpshooters may make as many jumps and captures as they can in one turn, as long as they land on vacant spaces after capturing each soldier. The captured soldiers are removed from the board. If one of the officers fails to make a possible jump and capture, it is removed from the board.

The foot soldiers may only move forward, diagonally, and sideways, but never backward. They may not jump officers but must try to trap them in the fortress or on the battlefield to win the game.

176

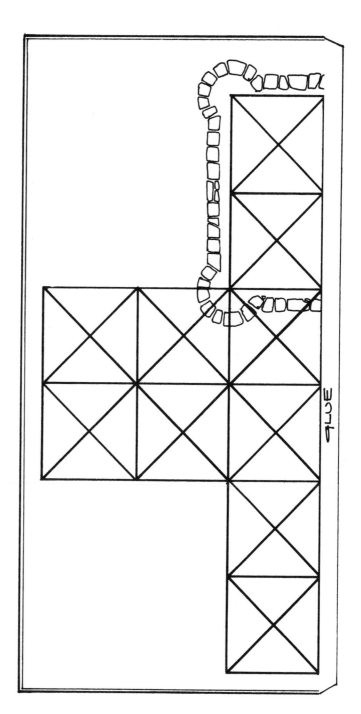

ASALTO PLAYING-
BOARD PATTERN.—I.

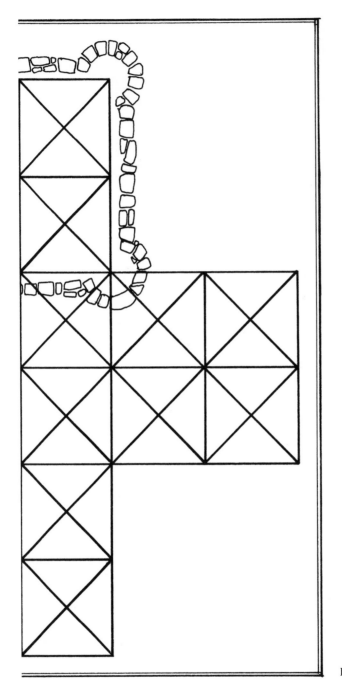

ASALTO PLAYING-
BOARD PATTERN.—2.

THE CHINESE REBEL GAME

THE CHINESE REBEL GAME, another battle game related to Fox and Geese, is played on a board like the one illustrated below. A Commander, who corresponds to the Fox, is placed in the center of the board. He attempts to evade the 20 Soldiers who surround him. Although he is outnumbered and heavily surrounded, the Commander may capture the Soldiers by jumping over them as in Fox and Geese.

CHINESE REBEL GAME BOARD FROM
THOMAS HYDE'S *DE LUDUS ORIENTALIBUS* (1694).

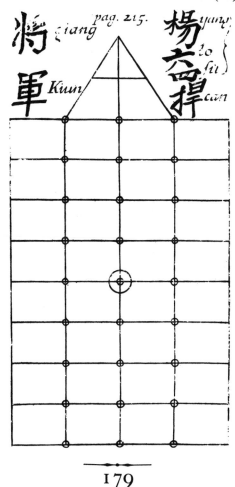

HOW TO PLAY THE CHINESE REBEL GAME.

NUMBER OF PLAYERS.—Two.

OBJECTIVE.—The Soldiers try to trap the Commander by surrounding him or penning him into a corner. The Commander may win by capturing so many Soldiers that it is impossible for them to surround him or by returning to his camp, which is marked by the *x* on the playing board.

MATERIALS.—A rectangular playing board of 39 spaces with a triangular area that surrounds the specially marked camp of the Commander at one end of the board, and 20 playing pieces of one color for the Soldiers and one piece of another color for the Commander.

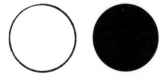

TO BEGIN PLAY.—The pieces are arranged as illustrated below.

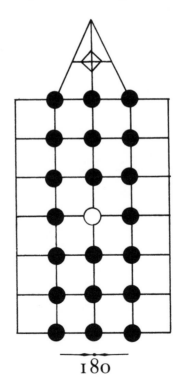

The players decide who is the Commander. The Commander takes the first turn and the players continue alternating turns.

To Play.—Both the Soldiers and the Commander may move forward, sideways, and backward into a vacant spot where the lines intersect, but neither can move diagonally. The Commander may capture a Soldier by jumping over it into the adjacent vacant spot. He may jump only one Soldier at a time. That Soldier is removed from the board when captured. The Commander will always capture a Soldier on his first move.

Since the Soldiers almost always win, unless the Commander is particularily cunning, it is suggested that the players alternate being the Commander and play a set of games to see who can trap the Commander the most number of times.

CHINESE REBEL GAME PLAYING-BOARD PATTERN.—I.

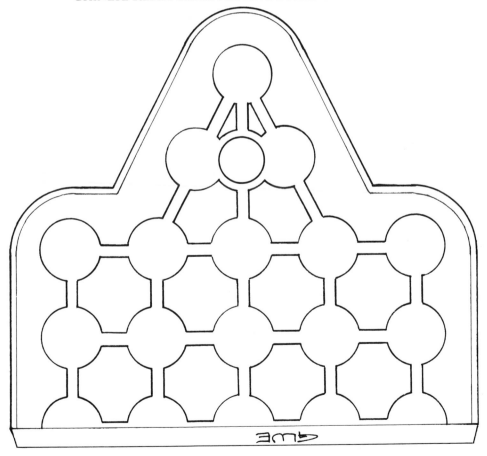

CHINESE REBEL GAME PLAYING-BOARD PATTERN.—2.

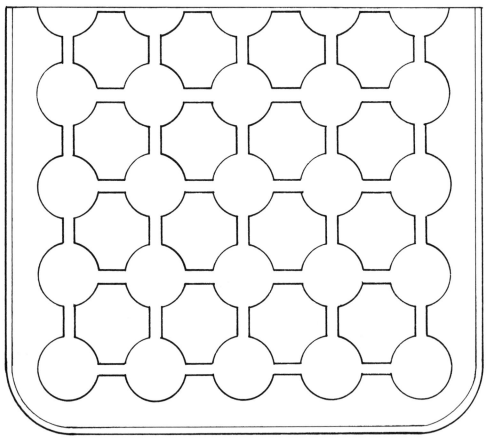

HARE AND HOUNDS

HARE AND HOUNDS is a modern variation of Fox and Geese that was first manufactured in England by the Chad Valley Game Company in 1922. As in Fox and Geese, a highly mobile player, the Hare, attempts to avoid capture by a pack of less mobile Hounds.

HOW TO PLAY
HARE AND HOUNDS.

NUMBER OF PLAYERS.—Two to six. One player is the Hare and the other players are the Hounds.

OBJECTIVE.—The Hare attempts to escape the Hounds and reach one of the two spaces marked with an *x* at one side of the board, while the Hounds attempt to capture the Hare by surrounding it so that it cannot move.

MATERIALS.—A square playing board that is marked with many circular spaces that are connected by lines. Five playing pieces of one color represent the Hounds and one piece of another color represents the Hare.

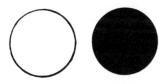

TO BEGIN PLAY.—The Hare is placed in the center space on the side of the board that has five playing spaces. The Hounds are placed in any five of the six playing spaces on the opposite side of the board.

TO PLAY.—The Hare always has the first move and may move one space in any direction in each turn.

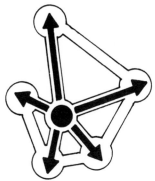

The Hounds also move one space per turn and can move in any direction except backwards.

The five Hounds may be moved in any order. If more than one player is moving the Hounds, these players must agree on which Hound is to be moved each turn.

The five Hounds try to win the game by surrounding and trapping the Hare so that it cannot move, as illustrated below.

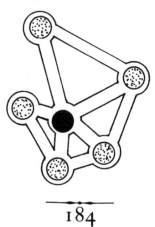

For the Hare to win the game, it must evade the Hounds and reach one of the spaces on the board marked with an *x*.

HARE AND HOUNDS PLAYING-BOARD PATTERN.—1.

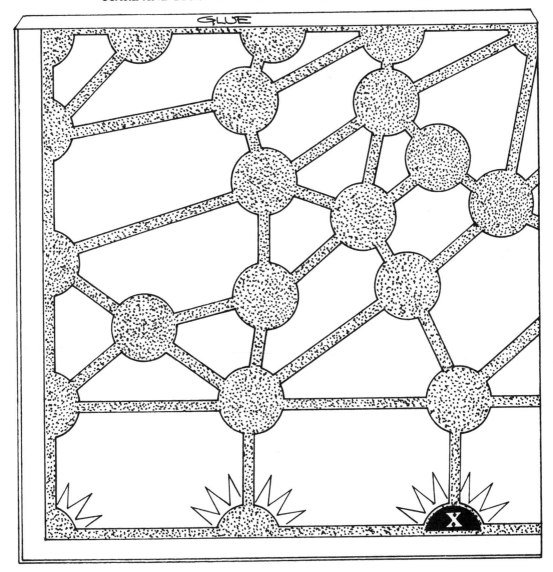

185

HARE AND HOUNDS PLAYING-BOARD PATTERN.—2.

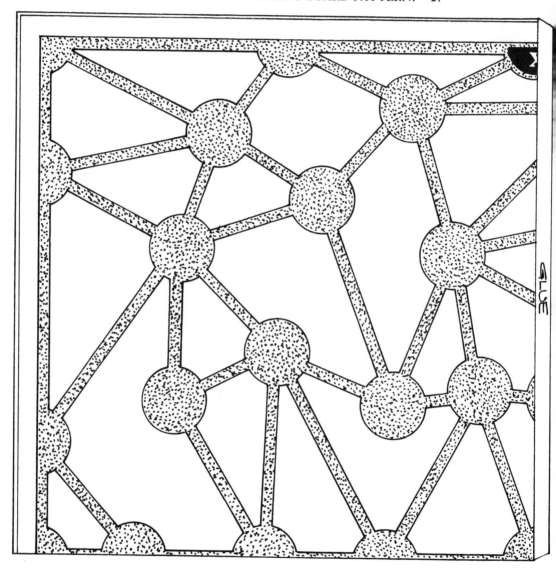

Hare and Hounds playing-board pattern.—3.

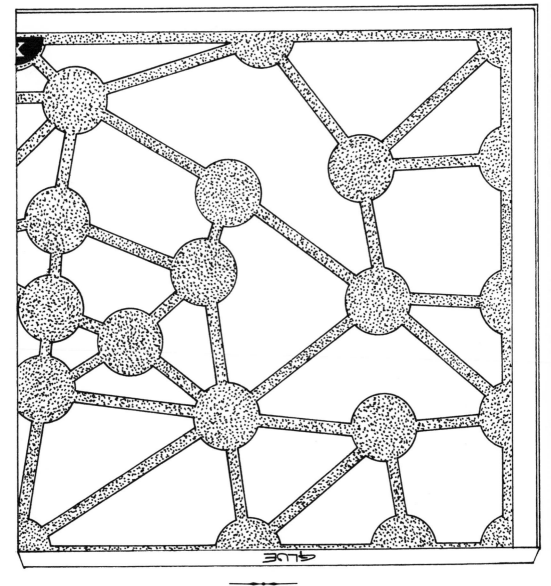

HARE AND HOUNDS PLAYING-BOARD PATTERN.—4.

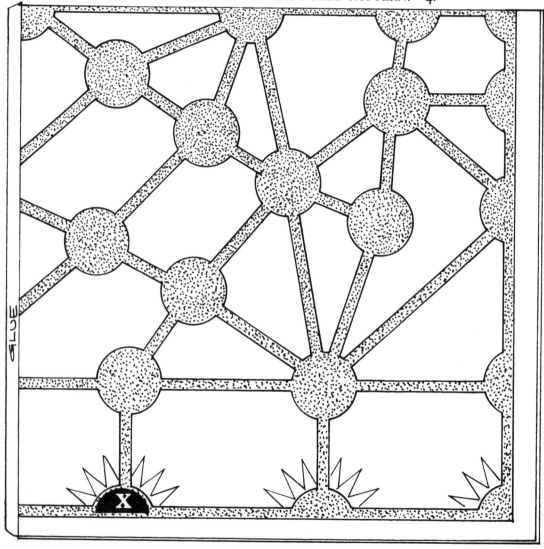

NYOUT

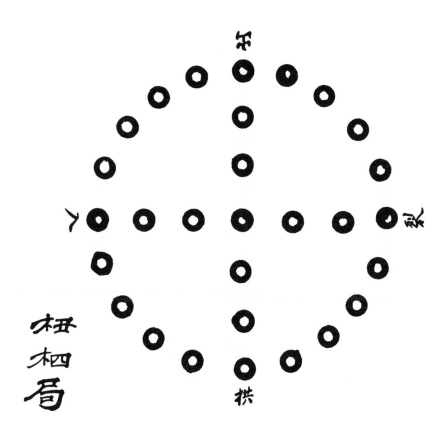

NYOUT, a cross-and-circle race game that has been played in Korea for hundreds of years, combines luck with unique possibilities to out-maneuver your opponent. The playing pieces are traditionally carved out of wood or ivory and are known as *mal*, or horse. The boards are often decorated with symbolic images in place of the circles commonly used today.

By the late nineteenth century, Nyout had also become a popular parlor game in the United States that was manufactured by Parker Brothers.

HOW TO PLAY NYOUT.

NUMBER OF PLAYERS.—Any number may play individually or in teams.

OBJECTIVE.—To be the first player to get all of your pieces, or "horses," around the board.

MATERIALS.—Nyout is played on a board marked with 20 colored circles forming a larger circle. Nine more circles form a cross in the interior of the larger circle. The circles at the center of the cross and at the North, South, East, and West points on the outer circle are larger than the others.

Each player has two, three, or four playing pieces of a different color from their opponent's pieces. It is up to the players to decide how many pieces they will play with.

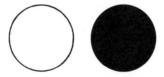

Traditionally, the game is played with flat strips of wood to determine moves up to a score of five, but a die may also be used.

TO BEGIN PLAY.—The players each throw the die, and the one throwing the highest number takes the first turn. Whenever a six is thrown, the player cannot use it and must roll again.

Each player enters his or her piece or pieces according to the number thrown. Horses are entered on the starting circle, which counts as one, and are moved around the board in a counterclockwise direction.

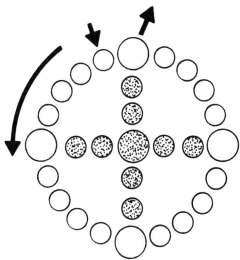

A player may have more than one piece on the ring at a time, and if partners are playing, each partner may move either his own pieces or the partner's pieces.

To Play.—Whenever a horse lands exactly on one of the larger circles, the player may move it on an alternate route along either the horizontal or vertical arms of the interior cross. These routes provide shortcuts to the exit circle or may allow a piece to evade an opponent's horse.

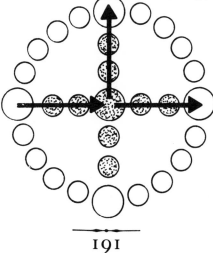

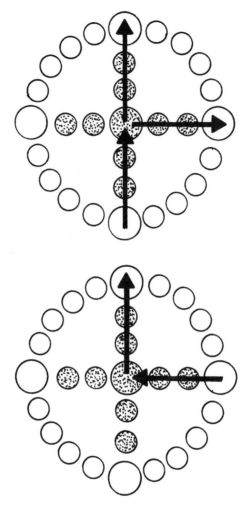

A player does not have to move a piece along an alternate route but may decide to continue along the outer ring of circles.

If a player's horse lands on a circle already occupied by an opponent's horse, the opponent's piece is captured and returned to the starting circle. The player is then allowed another roll of the die.

When a player's piece lands on a circle already occupied by one of that player's horses or one of the player's partner's horses, the two horses may be moved together as a "double piece" in any subsequent turn by the player or the partner.

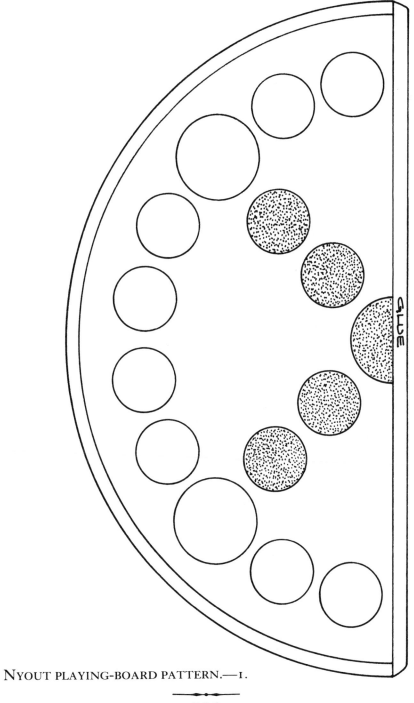

NYOUT PLAYING-BOARD PATTERN.—I.

193

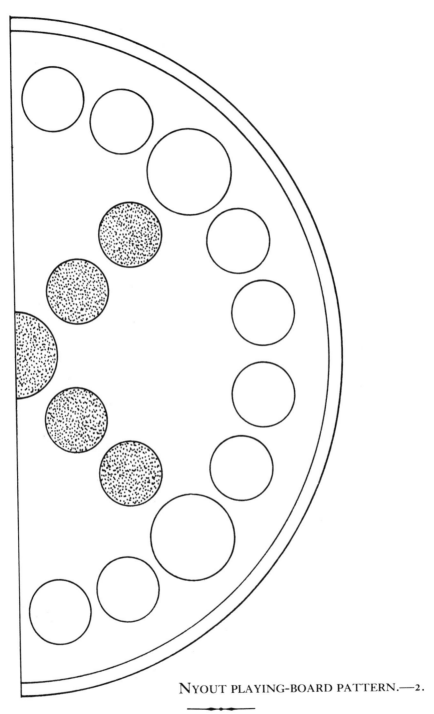

NYOUT PLAYING-BOARD PATTERN.—2.

DRAUGHTS

LOSER DRAUGHTS
DIAGONAL DRAUGHTS
CONTINENTAL DRAUGHTS
DRAUGHTS FOR THREE
REVERSI

Draughts, one of the all-time favorite two-player board games, combines a Chess board of 64 black and white squares with the pieces of medieval Backgammon and the moves of Alquerque. The simple rules can be learned in minutes, but the fast-moving game always provides exciting opportunities to block and out-maneuver your opponent.

Draughts originated about A.D. 1100 in southern France, where the pieces were called *Ferses*, after the name of the queen in the medieval game of Chess. The game itself was known as *Fierges*. But when the name of the Chess queen was changed to *Dame*, each piece in Draughts also became known as a *Dame* and the game as *Dames*.

When a rule making it compulsory to capture an opponent's piece became popular in France around 1535, two versions of the game emerged. The capturing game was known as *Jeu Forcé*, and the non-capturing game or non-huffing game as *Le Jeu Plaisant de Dames*, later simplified to *Plaisant*. The capturing game made its way in the sixteenth century to England, where it was called Draughts, and on to North America, where it is called Checkers.

Draughts was such a popular game during the nineteenth century that 27 different books on it were published in England alone between 1800 and 1895! One of the most famous of these books, the *Guide to the Game of Draughts, Containing 500 Select Games*, published by Joseph Sturges in 1800, summed up the universal fascination of Draughts:

> To ascertain, distinctly, consequences in their causes—to calculate with promptitude the result of intricate variety, to elude by vigilant caution the snares of stratagem, are lessons the game of Draughts strongly inculcates, and uniformly explains.

HOW TO PLAY DRAUGHTS.

NUMBER OF PLAYERS.—Two.

OBJECTIVE.—Each player tries to either: move the pieces so that the opponent is unable to make a move; or capture all of the opponent's pieces and remove hem from the playing board.

MATERIALS.—A square playing board of 64 dark and light squares. Both players have 12 playing pieces, each player having a different color.

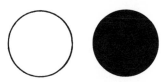

To Begin Play.—The game is played on the dark squares. The player with the dark pieces always takes the first turn, so the players must decide who will play with the dark pieces. Each player arranges the 12 pieces on the 12 dark squares in the first three rows on their side of the board.

Each player may move only one piece per turn. Once a player has touched a piece, it must be moved in that turn. The pieces are moved one square at a time, diagonally only. Pieces may not be moved backwards.

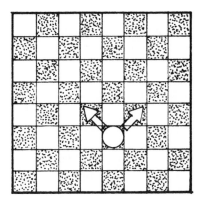

To Play.—An opponent's piece is captured when a piece jumps over it to a vacant square next to it. More than one piece may be captured each turn, as long as there is a vacant square to land on after each successive jump, as illustrated below, but a piece may not be jumped more than once.

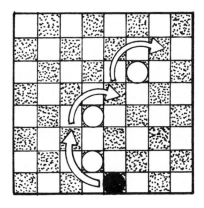

A player may have a choice of whether to capture a small or large number of pieces. But if the player decides to make the larger capture, all the possible jumps and captures must be completed. If a player has a choice between a non-capturing move and a capturing move, the capturing move must be taken. Failure to make a capturing move or to complete a capturing move can result in one of the following penalties:

- The opponent may request that the piece that has just made the move be returned to its original position and that the correct and complete move be made.

○ The opponent may let the move remain as made, but the piece that failed to make a capturing move must make that move in the player's next turn.

- Or, the opponent may choose to remove, or huff, the player's piece that has just made an incorrect move. This huff does not count as a turn, so the opponent gets to then make a move.

(In modern Checkers, these penalties have been revised to rule that the opponent should correct a wrong move and force the player to make it correctly before the game continues.)

Once a piece reaches the last row on the opponent's side of the board, it becomes a "king." The player's turn ends as the piece becomes a king, even if other jumps are possible. A king is "crowned" by a player's placing another piece of the same color on top of it. Once a piece becomes a king, it may be moved either forward or backward along the diagonal squares to a vacant square.

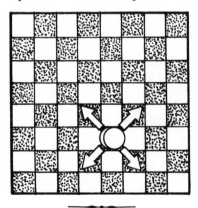

A king may be captured by either a regular piece or by another king piece.

If neither player can remove all the opponent's pieces or prevent the opponent from moving, then the game ends in a draw.

DRAUGHTS PLAYING-BOARD PATTERN.—I.

DRAUGHTS PLAYING-BOARD PATTERN.—2.

LOSER DRAUGHTS

LOSER DRAUGHTS is Draughts with a twist. The object is to lose the game! If a player can successfully place his or her pieces so that the opponent must jump them all and thus loses all of his or her pieces, then that player is the winner. You can also win by positioning your pieces so that it is impossible to move anywhere on the board.

Loser Draughts is played on a regular Draughts or Checkers board of 64 squares. Each player has 12 playing pieces of his or her own color that are placed on the board as in Draughts.

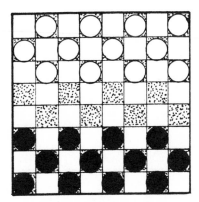

The same rules apply to Loser Draughts as do in Draughts except when a player fails to jump an opponent's piece. Instead of the player's piece being "huffed," or removed from the board, the opponent should request that the player make the jump and remove one or more of his (the opponent's) pieces. Likewise, if a player has several possible jump moves, the opponent may insist that the move that captures the most pieces is made since the opponent wants to lose as many pieces as possible in order to win the game.

DIAGONAL DRAUGHTS

DIAGONAL DRAUGHTS, one variation of Draughts, is played with the same board and rules as Draughts, but the playing pieces are positioned on diagonally opposite corners of the board. The game may be

played with nine pieces for each player, which are placed on the board as illustrated below.

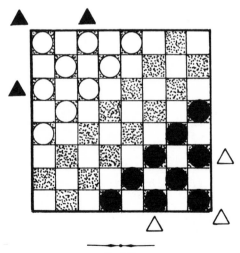

The squares marked with the triangles indicate the squares that must be reached by a piece from the opposite side of the board in order to be crowned a king.

The game may also be played with 12 pieces per player; they are placed on the board as illustrated below. The squares that must be reached in order to be crowned are also marked with triangles.

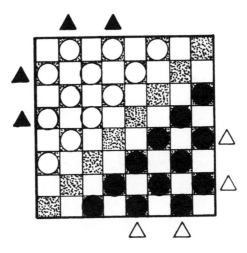

CONTINENTAL DRAUGHTS

CONTINENTAL or POLISH DRAUGHTS, considered one of the greatest two-player board games in the world, was first played in Paris in the 1720s. Various modifications in the rules for the game, which is played with 20 pieces for each player on a board of 100 squares, have made it a fast-moving battle that tests your ability to plan your moves in advance. The unique maneuverability of the king pieces, which can be moved diagonally any number of vacant squares, is especially exciting in this version of Draughts.

As in other Draughts games, the objective of Continental Draughts is to capture all of your opponent's pieces or to trap his or her pieces so that it is impossible for them to move.

To Begin Play.—Each player's 20 pieces are positioned on the board as illustrated below.

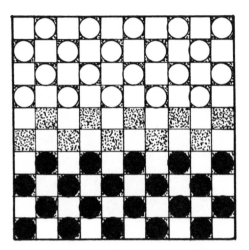

Each piece may be moved diagonally forward one square—except when jumping to capture, when a piece may jump both diagonally forward and backward, as illustrated below.

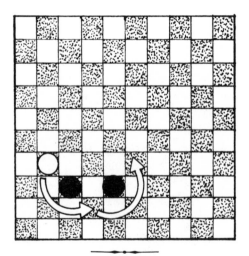

If a player has the choice of a small capture or a large capture, the larger capture must be made. If more than one capture of equal quantity is possible, the most damaging capture (one that includes a king, for instance) must be made.

A player's piece may be crowned a king when it reaches the opponent's back row and remains there at the end of a turn. If a piece reaches the back row but must continue moving on to complete captures, it cannot be crowned. It must wait until it lands on a square on the opponent's back row and remains there at the end of the move.

A piece that has been made a king has much more power than in regular Draughts, Checkers, or Diagonal Draughts. A king may be moved diagonally any number of vacant squares in one move, as illustrated below (left).

A king may also land on any diagonally vacant square, after capturing a piece, as illustrated below (right). An opponent's piece may be jumped only once within a capturing move.

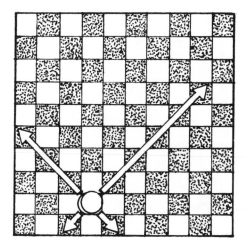

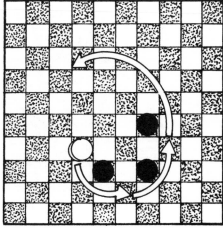

CONTINENTAL DRAUGHTS PLAYING-BOARD PATTERN.—I.

CONTINENTAL DRAUGHTS PLAYING-BOARD PATTERN.—2.

DRAUGHTS FOR THREE

DRAUGHTS FOR THREE was invented by an Englishman, John Hyde, and patented in the United States in 1888. Played by three people on a triangular board, the game requires even more concentration and strategy than Draughts because both the rules and the game are much more complicated.

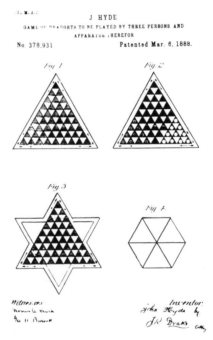

J HYDE
GAME OF DRAUGHTS TO BE PLAYED BY THREE PERSONS AND
APPARATUS THEREFOR
No. 378,931   Patented Mar. 6, 1888.

HOW TO PLAY DRAUGHTS FOR THREE.

NUMBER OF PLAYERS.—Three.

OBJECTIVE.—Each player tries to capture as many of the other two players' pieces as possible so that only one player is left in the game, becoming the winner.

MATERIALS.—A triangular-shaped playing board divided into 81 equilateral triangles, alternately dark and light. Each player uses ten playing pieces of his or her own color.

To Begin Play.—Each player places his or her ten pieces in the corners of the board on the dark triangles. The players decide who will take the first turn. All subsequent moves are taken in rotation

To Play.—Each player may move one piece one triangle (one space) per turn, toward either opponent's home base, as indicated by the arrows in the above illustration. The game is played on only the dark triangles.

A player crowns a piece once it reaches the last line of triangles (except for the triangle forming the corner of the board) of either of the opponent's home bases. Once a piece is crowned it may also move

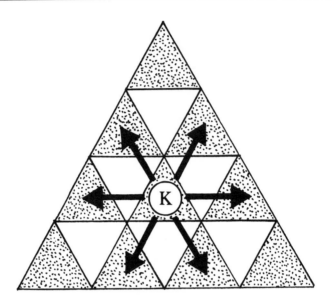

horizontally. The horizontal can be determined as being parallel to the base of the triangular board farthest from the piece's home base.

When a piece is crowned and becomes a king, it cannot be moved along the outer rows of the board until it has been moved in at least one space from the outer row. After being brought in, it may be moved back to an outer row, but each time it moves to the outer row, the king must be brought back to an inside row again.

As in Draughts, a piece may be captured by regular pieces and kings by being jumped. More than one piece may be jumped and captured in the same turn. If a player has a choice of jumping and capturing one or more pieces of either opponent, the choice is the player's. If a player fails to make a capturing jump, her piece may be "huffed," or removed from the board, as in regular Draughts.

After one player is out of the game, the player who succeeds in capturing the remaining opponent's last piece is the winner. If the two remaining players both have only a king left and they are unable to force each other into a position in which a king can be captured, the game is considered a draw. Likewise, if all three players are left with only a king and are unable to force the capture of their opponent's pieces, the game ends in a draw.

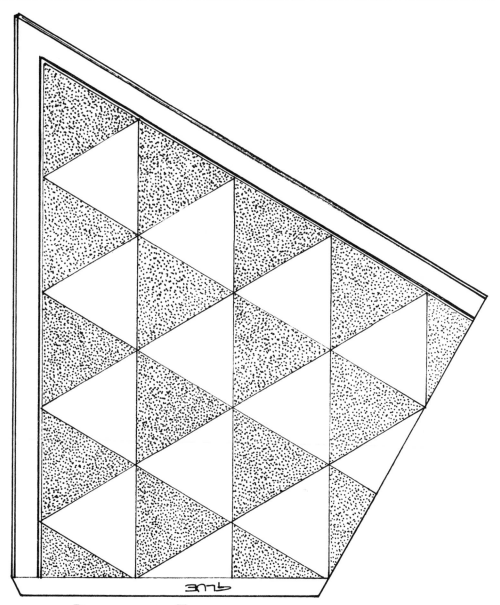

DRAUGHTS FOR THREE PLAYING-BOARD PATTERN.—1.

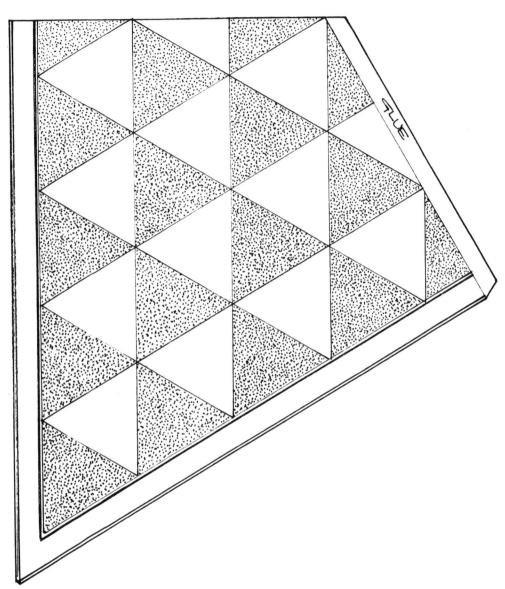

DRAUGHTS FOR THREE PLAYING-BOARD PATTERN.—2.

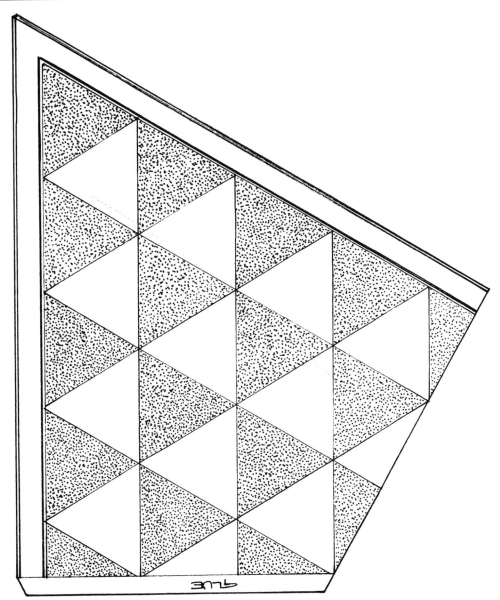

DRAUGHTS FOR THREE PLAYING-BOARD PATTERN.—3.

REVERSI

REVERSI, a board game for two that was invented in England in the late nineteenth century, is played on the Draughts or Checkers board of 64 squares. Even though the rules are as simple as in Draughts and take just a minute to learn, Reversi can take a lifetime to master!

Throughout Reversi, the players strategically place their pieces on the squares until the entire board is covered. But whenever one player outflanks one or more of the opponent's pieces, those pieces are reversed to the player's colors. Thus, Reversi is especially exciting as fortunes change and the colors of pieces are dramatically reversed throughout the game.

HOW TO PLAY REVERSI.

NUMBER OF PLAYERS.—Two.

OBJECTIVE.—To have more pieces of your own color on the board at the end of the game than your opponent does.

MATERIALS.—A Draughts board of 64 squares. Since the contrasting colors of the squares on a Draughts board have no significance in Reversi, you may find it less confusing to play the game on a grid of 64 plain squares and decide to make a board especially for Reversi, using the patterns provided. Sixty-four playing pieces, black on one side and white on the other, are used to play the game.

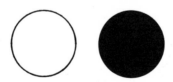

TO BEGIN PLAY.—Each player takes 32 pieces to use throughout the game. Determine which player is to take the first turn. Black always moves first. Each player places two pieces on the board in either of the two arrangements shown at the top of page 215.

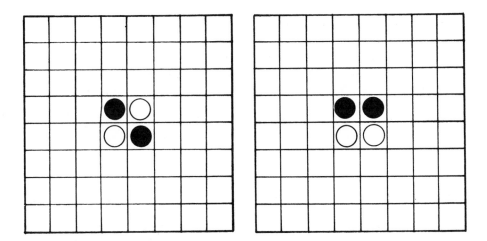

To Play.—Each player places one piece on the board at a time so that one or more of the opponent's pieces are bordered at each end, or "outflanked" by two of the player's own pieces. When one or more pieces are trapped by their being outflanked, they are reversed to show the color of their captor, as illustrated below.

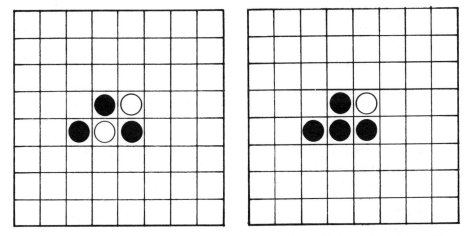

A player's piece may outflank any number of pieces in one turn. Any of the opponent's pieces that are in a row or continuous straight line may be outflanked. If the line is broken by one of the player's own

215

pieces or by a vacant square, it does not qualify as a continuous row and is not a correct move.

A player may outflank an opponent's pieces in any direction (diagonally, vertically, and horizontally) and in any number of directions in one turn, as shown in the following illustrations. In the first diagram, the white piece marked with the black square is the last piece placed on the board. Its position enables the player to outflank every one of the opponent's pieces and to reverse them to the player's own color!

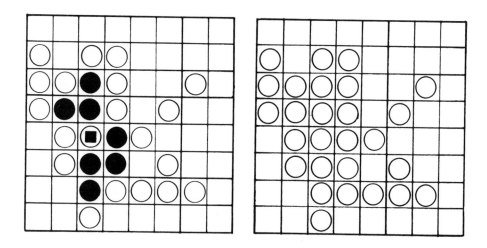

All the pieces that are outflanked in any move must be reversed even if not to the player's advantage. If a player mistakenly reverses a piece, or fails to reverse an outflanked piece, the mistake may be corrected if the opponent has not already moved. Otherwise, the pieces cannot be reversed and the mistake stands.

When a player cannot outflank at least one piece, his turn is forfeited. But if a player runs out of pieces and has the opportunity to outflank one of the opponent's pieces, the opponent must give the player a piece to make the move.

When all 64 pieces are on the board or when neither player can make a move, the game is over. The player with the most pieces on the board is the winner.

REVERSI PLAYING-BOARD PATTERN.—I.

REVERSI PLAYING-BOARD PATTERN.—2.

BACKGAMMON

THE POINTS GAME
THE DOUBLING GAME

Backgammon, a one-to-one battle, is one of the world's oldest games. In fact, Backgammon has been exciting and challenging board-game players for thousands of years. This intriguing game combines the luck of the dice with the calculating strategy of moving and positioning one's playing pieces. The rules are simple to learn—but the possibilities of combinations of moves are astounding!

The oldest known Backgammon board was one of five gaming boards found by Sir Leonard Woolley in the royal tombs at Ur in Iraq, which date from about 3000 B.C. Another version of the game, known in Persia and the Near East as *Nard*, is more than 1,600 years old. It is believed that Nard was introduced into Europe by the Arabs. Their game included a board with 24 points, 30 playing pieces, and a pair of dice.

Not only has Backgammon been played throughout history, but it has been popular all over the world as well. By the sixth century, the game was well known in China, where it was called *t'shu-p'u*. Both the Chinese and Japanese versions, *sunoroko*, are played on a circular board. Fifteen variations of the game are illustrated in the *Libro de Juegos* of King Alfonso X (1251–1282) of Castille. In fact, Backgammon appears in all sorts of writings from Plato and Sophocles to Chaucer's *Canterbury Tales*.

Originally, Backgammon was known by the Latin name *tabula*, which became "tables" when the game was introduced into England. Many other games that were played on a table, such as Chess, were at one time known as Tables. In Spain, Backgammon is called *tablas reales*, and in Italy, *tavole reale*, both references to "royal tables." Germans call the game *puff*, and the French game is known as *trictrac*.

LE TRICTRAC.

In the seventeenth century, the game became known as Back-gammon, since pieces are often required to go "back" and re-enter the board, or "gamen."

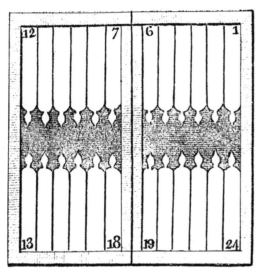

THE BACKGAMMON BOARD.

Since the Middle Ages, the Backgammon board has given crafts-men the opportunity to express their skill by making boards and pieces that are beautiful works of art, made out of inlaid woods, polished stones, silver, and gold leaf. As the game has experienced periodic re-vivals in popularity, improvements have been made in the board and dice. For example, in 1873, a folding Backgammon board was patented in the United States. In 1884, another American patented a Backgam-mon board and dice cup lined with soft material to muffle the rattling noise usually associated with the game.

Perhaps the greatest contribution Americans made to the game was the addition of the doubling cube during the 1920s, when Back-gammon was experiencing another surge in popularity. Not only is the cube a lethal weapon with which to bluff an opponent, but it also en-hances the gambling possibilities of the game. This associaton of Backgammon with gambling is not new. In the seventh century the game was declared illegal by Emperor Jito of Japan, and throughout the Middle Ages, the Catholic church also tried to prohibit it. Today, the doubling cube remains an important part of modern Backgammon sets, which are usually portable sets that can be carried around and played anywhere, just as the game was carried by the Crusaders more than 800 years ago!

(No Model.)

A. A. JACKSON.
GAME BOARD, DICE BOX, &c.

No. 296,012.   Patented Apr. 1, 1884.

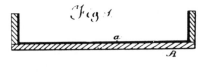

Fig 1.

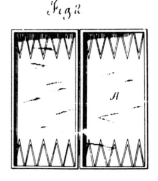

Fig 2.

Fig. 3.

Witnesses: Inventor
Tom A. Rosenbaum   A. Amelia Jackson
Wm M. Stockbridge.   by V. D. Stockbridge
                              atty

HOW TO PLAY BACKGAMMON.

NUMBER OF PLAYERS.—Two.

OBJECTIVE.—To be the first player to move all of your pieces to your inner table, where they can be removed (borne off) from the board. The first player to "bear off" all his or her pieces from the board wins.

MATERIALS.—A rectangular board consisting of 24 points, or elongated triangles of alternating colors. A "bar" divides the board down the middle. Players sit on opposite sides of the board. Their first six points are called their "inner table." Points seven through 12 are the player's "outer table."

Each player has 15 pieces of a different color from their opponent's pieces. Two pairs of dice are used to determine moves, and sometimes dicing cups are also used to throw the dice.

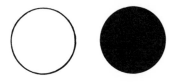

TO BEGIN PLAY.—Pieces are placed on the board as illustrated below. Traditionally, the inner tables are always nearer the source of light.

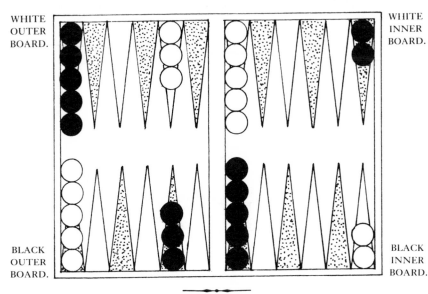

Each player rolls a single die. The player rolling the highest number goes first, choosing which side of the board and color of pieces to play with. This player moves first, combining the two single throws of the players as her first move. Throughout the rest of the game, each player both throws the die and moves accordingly in alternating turns.

The two numbers of the two dice thrown each turn may be used separately to move two pieces or combined to move one piece. For example, with a throw of "four" and "two," a player may move: one piece two points and then move the same piece another four points; one piece four points and then the same piece two more points; or two pieces, one for two points and one for four points in either of the possible combinations.

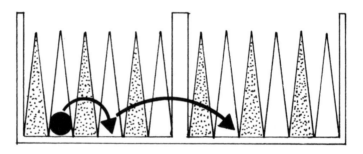

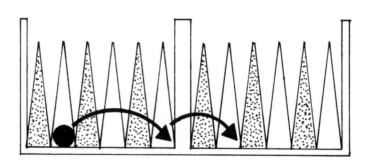

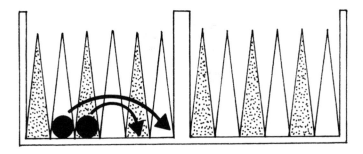

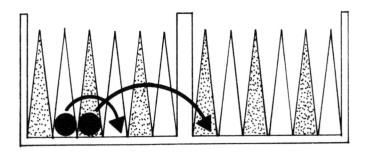

A player's pieces may be moved to any point except one already occupied by two or more of the opponent's pieces. When a player has two or more pieces on a point, this is called "making a point," and the opponent is barred from landing on that point. If one piece is being moved both the numbers thrown, neither count may land on a point "made" by the opponent's pieces.

If a player throws a pair, this throw is known as a "doublet," and the player is allowed to move double the number thrown. For example, if a "five" and a "five" are thrown, the player is allowed to move five, five, five, and five. The player may use the four fives in any combination.

A player must always use both numbers thrown whenever possible, but if a player can use only one of the numbers on the pair of dice, and there is a choice, the highest number must always be used. Any part of the throw that cannot be used is lost.

The two players move their pieces in opposite directions. For example, white would move from black's inner board to black's outer board, then on to white's outer board and, at last, to white's inner board or home.

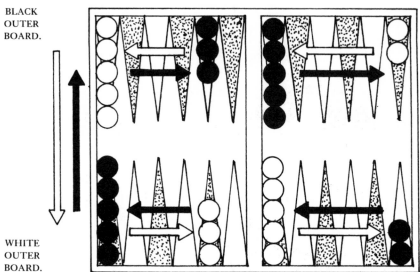

BLACK
OUTER
BOARD.

BLACK
INNER
BOARD.

WHITE
OUTER
BOARD.

WHITE
INNER
BOARD.

When all of a player's pieces are in his or her inner board, or home, then this player may begin to "bear off."

TO PLAY.—When a single piece occupies a point, this is known as a "blot." If the opponent lands on this blot, the piece is removed from the board and placed on the "bar," where it must remain until it can be entered into the opponent's inner board.

A player must re-enter any pieces from the bar before any other moves may be made. A piece may enter the board on points of the same number as shown on the dice. For example, if a "five" and "three" are thrown, a piece may be entered on a five point or a three

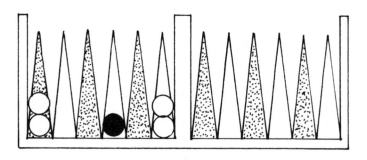

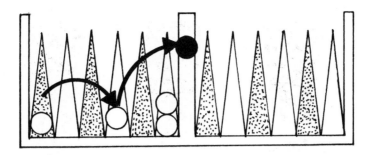

point in the opponent's inner board. If a point is made by two or more of the opponent's pieces, a player may not enter on that point. If all six of an opponent's inner-board points are made, the player forfeits that turn until the opponent's plays open up the inner board and make entry possible.

A player may land on two or more blots in the same throw. Likewise, a player has the choice of landing on a blot or not landing on it unless no other move is possible.

A player may begin to bear off pieces when all 15 pieces are on points in that player's inner board area. The numbers thrown on the dice may be used to bear off a piece or to move it forward, or both. If a number higher than any point occupied by the player's pieces is thrown, a piece from the highest point is borne off. If a number is thrown for any points not covered by pieces and it is not sufficient to bear off a piece, then a piece from the highest point (farthest point) may be moved forward. Four pieces may be borne off at the same time with a doublet.

If a player's blot is hit by the opponent while the player is bearing off, the piece must be entered from the bar and moved around the board to the player's inner board before any more pieces may be borne off.

Traditionally, the winner of a game of Backgammon may "score" the victory in the following manner:

A "single game"—if the opponent has borne off at least one piece and has no pieces in the winner's inner board.

A "double game" or "gammon"—if the opponent has not borne off any pieces.

A "triple game" or "backgammon"—if the opponent has not borne off any pieces and has at least one piece still on the bar or in the winner's inner board.

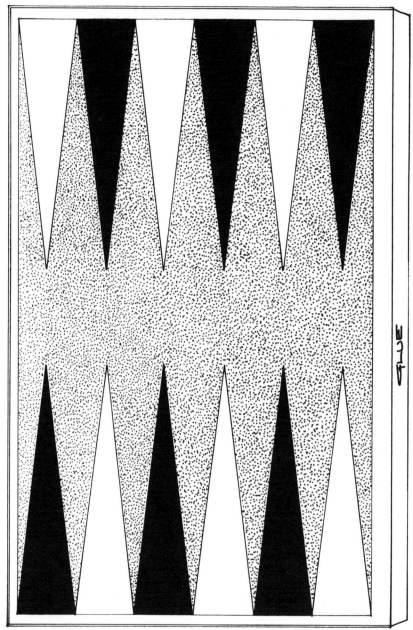

BACKGAMMON PLAYING-BOARD PATTERN.—1.

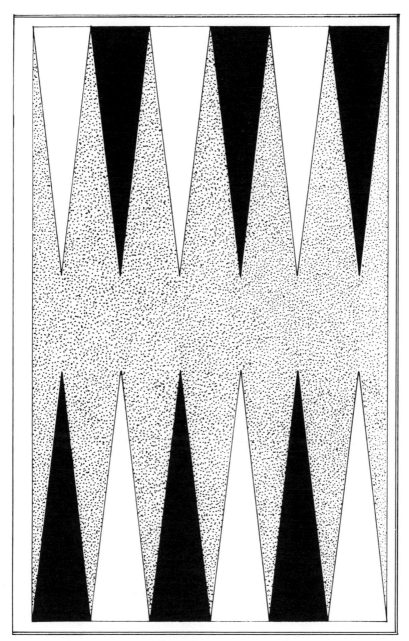

BACKGAMMON PLAYING-BOARD PATTERN—2.

THE POINTS GAME

THE POINTS GAME of Backgammon is another way to play the game with degrees of victory. The winner gets four points for each of the opponent's pieces still in the winner's inner board or on the bar, three points for each of the opponent's pieces in the winner's outer board, two points for each of the opponent's pieces in the opponent's outer board, and one point for each of the opponent's pieces in the opponent's inner board. If the opponent has not borne off any pieces, the score is doubled for a gammon. If the opponent has not borne off any pieces and has at least one piece still on the bar or in the winner's inner board, the score is tripled for a backgammon.

THE DOUBLING GAME

THE DOUBLING GAME is another way to play Backgammon, and it was invented in the United States during the 1920s. The doubling cube is a large die with the numbers 2:4:8:16:32:64 on its sides.

Throughout the game, the stakes may be doubled and redoubled in addition to the traditional double for a gammon and a triple score for a backgammon.

At the beginning of the game, the doubling cube is placed with the number "64" up to denote a value of one. If matching numbers are thrown by the two players when they are throwing the die to determine who is the first player, the cube is usually automatically doubled to "2." It is up to the players to decide if they will allow only one such automatic doubling of the cube or how many times they want this to happen.

Throughout the game, each player has the right to offer the first voluntary doubling of the cube to the opponent. If the opponent accepts, the cube is doubled. If not, the opponent forfeits the game at the stakes represented by the present number on the cube. A player must offer the doubling cube to an opponent before the dice are thrown for his turn.

After the first voluntary doubling of the cube, a player may only offer the doubling cube if the opponent made the previous doubling offer. Thus it is possible for a player to win a game with stakes as high as "192"—if the doubling cube has been doubled to "64" and then the player wins a Backgammon, which automatically triples the "64" to "192"!

HISTORICAL ILLUSTRATIONS (SOURCES)

The historical illustrations used in *Play It Again* are drawn primarily from works published during the nineteenth century. In addition to children's magazines and books, sources for the illustrations include patents, rule books, and classic works on board games, as well as the board games themselves. The following references will, we hope, be of use to those interested in doing further research on the history of board games.

ii ☺ Board games.   Hermann Wagner, *Speilbuch für Knaben* (Leipzig and Berlin: Otto Spamer, 1885), figs. 208–212.

4 ● Dice.   Jacques Stella, *Games and Pastimes of Childhood* (Facsimile of the 1657 edition reprinted by Dover Books: New York, 1969), pl. 37.

4 ☺ Dice-Play.   Charles Hoole (trans.), *Orbis Sensualium Pictus*, Jan Amos Comenius (London: F. Kirton, 1659), p. 272, pl. cxxxiv.

5 ● Dice and Dicing Cup.   *Backgammon: Its History and Practice*, "By the Author of 'Whist' " (London: D. Bogue, 1844), title page.

5 ☺ Le Toton.   L. Harquevaux and L. Pelletier, *200 Jeux D'Enfants* (Paris: Librairie Larousse, n.d.), p. 161.

10 ● Checkers.   (William Clarke), *Boy's Own Book* (New York: C. S. Francis & Co., 1855), n.p.

13 ⊜ Game Boards, Dice, and Dicing Cups. *Harrod's Catalogue,* 1895, p. 1302.

19 ● "The Royal and Entertaining Game of Goose," Courtesy of the Yale Center for British Art, folio A, G1.

20 ⊜ Nineteenth-century Game of Goose board. L. Harquevaux and L. Pelletier, *200 Jeux D'Enfants* (Paris: Librairie Larousse, n.d.), p. 166.

21 ● Children playing the Game of Goose. L. Harquevaux and L. Pelletier, *200 Jeux D'Enfants* (Paris: Librairie Larousse, n.d.), p. 167.

29 ⊜ Le Merelle and Le Cerf Volant. Jacques Stella, *Games and Pastimes of Childhood* (Facsimile of the 1657 edition reprinted by Dover Books: New York, 1969), pl. 17.

30 ● Morrice Board. Miss Leslie (Eliza), *The American Girl's Book* (New York: James Miller, 1851), p. 148.

31 ⊜ Game board. R. Creifelds, U.S. Patent No. 52,784. Patented December 24, 1918.

37 ● Game board. J. J. Donahue and J. H. Sullivan, U.S. Patent No. 25,349. Patented April 7, 1896.

41 ⊜ De Indorum Ludo Tchupur. Thomas Hyde, *De Ludis Orientalibus* (London: 1694), p. 68. Courtesy of the Beinecke Library, Yale University.

42 ● Pachisi board in the courtyard of Futteypore Sikri Palace. Edward Falkener, *Games Ancient and Oriental* (London: Longmans, Green & Co., 1892), p. 257.

43 ⊜ Pachisi. Sears, Roebuck & Co. Catalogue, 1908, p. 1046.

53 ● Box lid for Snakes and Ladders game, manufactured in 1911 by the Chad Valley Company, England. From the Brian Love collection, as reproduced in *Play the Game* (Los Angeles: Reed Books, 1978), p. 91.

61 ⊜ Knights playing Alquerque. Alfonso X, *Das spanische schachzabelbuch des königs Alfons des Weisen vom jahre 1283* (Leipzig: K. W. Hiersemann, 1913), 91 Verso, pl. CLXXXII.

85 ● Solitaire. Gaston Tissandier, *Popular Scientific Recreations*, trans. Henry Frith (New York: Ward, Lock and Co., 1890[?]), p. 739.

91 ◒ Halma advertisement from the early 1890s.

100 ● Game board. J. E. Huffaker, U.S. Patent No. 2,235,615. Patented March 18, 1941.

109 ◒ Turkish Girls Playing Mancala. Stewart Culin, "Mancala, The National Game of Africa," *United States National Museum Report*, 1894, pl. 1.

110 ● Mancala Board, Maldive Islands. Stewart Culin, "Mancala, The National Game of Africa," *United States National Museum Report*, 1894, p. 599, fig. 5.

115 ◒ Game board. M. B. Lorenzana, et al., U.S. Patent No. 162,-742. Patented April 3, 1951.

119 ● Das Wettrennspiel. Hugo Elm, *Speil und Beihaftigung* (Dresden: Verlag von A. Müller-Fröbelhaus, 1892), p. 283, fig. 371.

120 ◒ Game of Steeple Chase. In the *Butler Brothers Catalogue*, 1914, p. 189.

120 ● Race for the Cup, *Butler Brothers Catalogue*, 1914, p. 189.

129 ◒ Queen's Guard boards. John D. Champlin and Arthur E. Bostwick, *The Young Folks Cyclopedia of Games and Sports* (New York: Henry Holt & Co., 1899), p. 1.

137 ● Game of Chivalry. *Butler Brothers Catalogue*, 1895, p. 99.

138 ◒ Game. G. S. Parker, U.S. Patent No. 1,780,038. Patented October 28, 1930.

147 ● Game board. W. B. Silver, U.S. Patent No. 255,892. Patented April 4, 1882.

161 ◒ Seega—the Modern Egyptian Game. Edward Falkener, *Games Ancient and Oriental* (London: Longmans, Green and Co., 1892), p. 63.

167 ● Sedentary Games. Joseph Strutt, *The Sports and Pastimes of the People of England*. Revision of the 1801 edition by J. Charles Cox (London: Methuen & Co., 1903), pl. XXXIII.

168 ☉ Playground Fox and Geese. John D. Champlin and Arthur E. Bostwick, *The Young Folks Cyclopedia of Games and Sports* (New York: Henry Holt & Co., 1899), p. 363, fig. 5.

174 ● Asalto. Hermann Wagner, *Speilbuch für Knaben* (Leipzig and Berlin: Otto Spamer, 1885), p. 255.

175 ☉ Siege. *Gamages Christmas Bazaar Catalogue*, 1913, p. 216.

179 ● Subjugatio Rebellium. Thomas Hyde, *De Ludis Orientalibus* (London: 1694), p. 215. Courtesy of the Beinecke Library, Yale University.

189 ☉ Nyout Playing Board. Stewart Culin, *Korean Games with Notes on the Corresponding Games of China and Japan* (Philadelphia: University of Pennsylvania, 1895), p. 67, fig. 75.

195 ● Draughts. *Every Boy's Book* (London and New York: George Routledge & Sons, 1868), p. 689.

201 ☉ Draughts. *The Boy's Own Book*. Seventh Edition (London: Vizetelly, Branston and Co., 1831), p. 305.

202 ● Draughts. *The Boy's Treasury of Sports, Pastimes and Recreations* (Philadelphia: Lea and Blanchard, 1847), p. 275.

203 ☉ Draughts. Miss Leslie (Eliza), *The American Girl's Book* (New York: James Miller, 1851), p. 142.

208 ● Game of Draughts to Be Played by Three Persons. J. Hyde, U.S. Patent No. 378,931. Patented March 6, 1888.

219 ☉ Backgammon table from fourteenth-century manuscript. Joseph Strutt, *The Sports and Pastimes of the People of England*. Revision of the 1801 edition by J. Charles Cox (London: Methuen & Co., 1903), pl. XXXIV.

220 ● Le Trictrac. Fréderic Dillaye, *Les Jeux de La Jeunesse* (Paris: Librairie Hackette et Cie, 1885), p. 325.

221 ☉ Sedentary Games. Joseph Strutt, *The Sports and Pastimes of the People of England*. Revision of the 1801 edition by J. Charles Cox (London: Methuen & Co., 1903), pl. XXXIII.

222 ● Game Board, Dice Box, etc.   A. A. Jackson, U.S. Patent No. 296,012. Patented April 1, 1884.

230 ☻ Backgammon.   *Backgammon: Its History and Practice.* "By the Author of 'Whist' " (London: D. Bogue, 1844), p. B.

INDEX